healing from heaven

Lilian B. Yeomans, M.D.

11th Printing 2001

International Standard Book Number 0-88243-730-5

Printed in the United States of America

Gospel Publishing House
Springfield, Missouri 65802-1894

Foreword

This little book, a reprint of lectures on divine healing delivered to students in the classroom and issued in this form in compliance with numerous requests, is called *Healing from Heaven* because it tells of eternal life brought down to man by the Son of God, which makes all who will accept it as freely as it is given conquerors, here and now, over sin and sickness. "The law of the Spirit of life in Christ Jesus hath made me free from the law of sin and death" (Romans 8:2). Disease is death begun, a death process.

I once called on a doctor at his office by invitation to discuss the teaching of the Scriptures on healing, and in taking my seat I accidentally knocked some medicine bottles off a shelf beside me. Laughingly apologizing for the mischance, I said, "Perhaps I shall knock them all down before I get through"; and my words were prophetic, for after taking a few doses of "healing from heaven" out of the Word, the doctor felt no further need of earthly remedies for himself or others but devoted the remainder of his life to presenting the claims of the Physician who has never lost a case — Jehovah-rapha.

Trusting that many others may be induced to taste and see that the Lord is good, this message is prayerfully sent forth.

LILIAN B. YEOMANS, M.D.

Contents

1

How I Was Delivered from Drug Addiction

Out of the depths have I cried unto Thee, O Lord.
Lord, hear my voice:
Let Thine ears be attentive
To the voice of my supplications.
If Thou, Lord, shouldest mark iniquities,
O Lord, who shall stand?
But there is forgiveness with Thee,
That Thou mayest be feared.
I wait for the Lord, my soul, doth wait,
And in His Word do I hope.
My soul waiteth for the Lord
More than they that watch for the morning:
I say, more than they that watch for the morning.
Let Israel hope in the Lord:
For with the Lord there is mercy,
And with Him there is plenteous redemption.
And He shall redeem Israel
From all his iniquities. — Psalm 130.

Out of the depths He lifted me! Abyss calls to
abyss, deep answers to deep. Only those who know
what it is to be bound as I was, captive of the mighty,

the prey of the terrible, will be able to understand how great was the deliverance which God wrought in me when He set me completely free from the degrading bondage of the morphine and chloral habits to which I had been a slave for years.

Sitting in darkness and in the shadow of death, bound in affliction and iron, I cried unto the Lord in my trouble and He saved me out of my distress, brought me out of darkness and the shadow of death, and broke my bands asunder. Do you not think that I have reason to praise God and glorify with every breath our all-conquering Jesus?

My sad story has a glad ending. But if anyone asks me how I contracted the morphine habit and became a drug addict, I can only say, "Through my fault, through my fault, through my most grievous fault."

I had been saved several years before; but, like Peter at one stage of his career, I was following afar off when I fell into this snare. It is a dangerous thing to follow afar off; I proved that to my cost.

Of course it is needless to say that nothing was further from my thought than becoming a drug addict. But I was engaged in very strenuous work, practicing medicine and surgery; and in times of excessive strain from anxiety or overwork, I occasionally resorted to morphine, singly or in combination with other drugs, to steady my nerves and enable me to sleep.

Knowing as I did the awful power of the habit-inducing drug to enslave and destroy its victims and with practical demonstrations of it before my eyes every day among the most brilliant members of the medical profession (I am a graduate of the University of Michigan Department of Medicine, Ann Arbor, Michigan), I was utterly inexcusable for daring to trifle even for a moment with such a destructive agent. And, alas! I thought I was toying with the drug but one day I made the startling discovery that the drug, or rather the demon power back of the drug, was playing with me. The bloodthirsty tiger that had devoured so many victims had me in his grasp.

Of the anguish of my soul the day I had to acknowledge to myself that morphine was the master and I the slave, I can even now hardly bear to speak.

I have this fault to find with many testimonies to healing — that the individual in telling of his healing, fails to make it clear that he (the witness) really suffered from the disease of which he professes to have been cured. It may be quite evident that he believes that he so suffered, but that is worlds away from the point at issue.

Testimonies of this character are quite valueless from a scientific standpoint; and to avoid falling into this error, I desire to leave no shadow of doubt on the mind of anyone that I was a veritable victim of morphinomania.

My ordinary dose of the drug varied from ten to fourteen grains a day. I thus took regularly about fifty times the normal dose for an adult man. I also took chloral hydrate, a most deadly drug used by criminals in the concoction of the so-called "knockout drops," taking one hundred and twenty grains in two doses of sixty grains at an interval of one hour each night at bedtime. The safe dose of chloral (indeed there is no safe dose in my opinion) is only about five grains, so I regularly took about twenty-four times what would be prescribed by a doctor.

I took the morphine by mouth, in the form of the sulphate, in one-half grain tablets, which I imported wholesale (I was living in Canada at this time) for my personal use.

While some have taken larger doses than this, I find it hard to believe that anyone was ever more completely enthralled by the drug than was I. I could by desperate efforts — only God knows how desperate they were — diminish the dose somewhat, but I always reached a minimum beyond which it was impossible to carry the reduction.

To ask me whether I had taken the drug on any particular day was as needless as to inquire whether I had inhaled atmospheric air; one seemed as necessary to my existence as the other.

When by tremendous exercise of will power I abstained from it for twenty-four hours, my condition was truly pitiable. I trembled with weakness; my whole body was bathed in cold sweat; my heart palpitated and fluttered; my respiration was irregular; my stomach was unable to retain even so much as a drop of water; my intestines were racked with pain and tortured with persistent diarrhea; I was unable to stand erect, to articulate clearly, or even sign my own name; my thoughts were unconnected; my mind was filled with horrid imaginings and awful forebodings. And worst of all, my whole being was possessed with the specific, irresistible, indescribable craving for the drug. Anyone who has not felt it cannot imagine what it is. Every cell of your body seems to be shrieking for it. It established a periodicity for itself in my case and I found that at five o'clock each afternoon *I had to have it!* The demand for it was imperative and could not be denied. I believe I would have known the time by the call if I had been in mid-ocean without watch or clock.

Say what you may about will power; for my part I am satisfied that no human determination can withstand the morphine demon when once his rule is established. His diabolical power is superhuman. But thank God! One has said, "I have given you power over all the power of the enemy." Divine power is to be had for the asking and receiving.

I did not succumb, however, without many fierce struggles. I believe I made at least fifty-seven desperate attempts to rid myself of the horrible incubus. Over and over again I threw away large quantities of the drugs, determined that I would never touch them again even if I died as the result of abstaining from them. I must have wasted a small fortune in this way. I tried all the substitutes recommended by the medical profession. I consulted many physicians, some of them men of national reputation. I can never forget the tender consideration which I received at the hands of some of these, but they were powerless to break my fetters. I got so far away from God that I actually tried Christian Science, falsely so-called. I also took the then famous Keeley Gold Cure. If there is anything I did not try I have yet to learn what it is.

I left the Gold Cure Institute in a crazed condition and was transferred to a sanitorium for nervous diseases and placed under the care of a famous specialist. From this institution I emerged still taking morphine and chloral, as the doctors would not allow me to dispense with them, partly because of my physical condition and more perhaps because of my unbalanced mental state, which always became aggravated when I no longer used them. Of the suffering these efforts to free myself cost me I would rather not speak.

I was a perfect wreck mentally and physically. "Like a skeleton with a devil inside," one of my nurses said; and I think her description, if not very flattering, was accurate enough. My friends had lost all hope of ever seeing me delivered; and, far from urging me to give up the drugs, advised me to take them as the only means of preserving the little reason that remained to me. They expected my wretched life to come to an early close and really could not desire to see so miserable an existence prolonged.

Perhaps many of us know "The Raven," that weird poem of Edgar Allen Poe's. The author, though he has been called the prince of American poets, perished miserably at a very early age as the result of addictions such as mine. In this poem he represents himself as opening his door to a black raven, a foul bird of prey. Once admitted, the raven resists all efforts to eject him but perches himself on a marble bust over the entrance and gazes at the poet with the eyes of a demon. Each time he is commanded to depart he croaks out the ominous word, "Nevermore."

> "Take thy beak from out my heart
>   And thy form from off my door."
>   Quoth the raven, "Nevermore."
> And the raven never flitting,
>   Still is sitting, still is sitting,
> On the pallid bust of Pallas,
>   Just above my chamber door,
> And his eyes have all the seeming
>   Of a demon's that is dreaming,
>   And his form from off my door,
> And his shadow from my heart,
> Shall be lifted
>   "Nevermore."

The poem is a parable in which the writer tells of his cruel and hopeless bondage to evil habits. It used to haunt me when I too was bound, and again and again Satan whispered to my tortured brain the awful word, "Nevermore."

Though I dreamed night and day of freedom, the dream seemed impossible of realization. I said, "It will take something stronger than death to deliver me, for the hold of the hideous thing is far deeper than my physical being." And I was right, for it took the law of the Spirit of Life in Christ Jesus which makes us free from the law of sin and death.

Do you ask, "Did you not pray?" Yes, I came to the place where I did nothing else. I prayed and prayed and prayed and prayed. Night after night I walked up and down our long drawing rooms calling on God, and sometimes almost literally tearing the hair out of my head. And you say, "And you weren't healed after that?" No, I wasn't healed because I didn't believe the simple statement of the Word of God; rather, my healing could not be manifested because of my unbelief. I shut the door and prevented the power of God from operating unhindered in my body.

"And why did you not have faith?" Simply because I did not have light enough to take it. It is a gift and must be appropriated. And moreover, God's method of bestowing it is through His Word. "Faith cometh" — note that it cometh — "by hearing, and hearing by the Word of God" (Romans 10:17).

I was getting very weak and spent hour after hour in bed, and God in His mercy kept me much alone so that He could talk to me. At last I drew my neglected Bible to me and plunged into it with full pur-

pose of heart to get all there was for me, to do all
that God told me to do, to believe all He said; and
praise God! the insoluble problem was solved, the
impossible was achieved, the deliverance was
wrought. There is no trouble about it when God can
get us to meet His conditions of repentance and
faith. When God says faith, He means *faith*. It is
well to know that.

If anyone asks by what special Scripture verse I
was healed, I feel as though I could almost say I was
healed by the whole Book. For it is there in Job,
the oldest book of the Bible, that has as clear teaching on healing in the Atonement as the Word contains (Job 33:24). In Genesis God made man as He
wanted him, in His own image and likeness, even as
to his physical being free from every disability. You'll
find healing in Exodus when the people of God
marched out of Egypt; for in Psalm 105:37 we read
that they marched out "with not one feeble person
among their tribes." Think of it! What a glorious procession. How did they do it? Through the wonder-
working power of the blood of the Passover Lamb.
Read about it in Leviticus in the leper-cleansing ceremony where the leper, when he had not a sound spot
in his entire body, was healed by the blood of the
bird slain over running water in an earthen vessel —
which is a picture of Christ, who through the Eternal
Spirit offered Himself without spot unto God. In Numbers every recorded case of sickness is dealt with by
supernatural means, prayer, sacrifice, and atonement.
In Deuteronomy God explicitly promised to take away
all sickness from His obedient people.

Suffice it to say I found a great number of healing passages in the Bible. And when God's words

were found, I "ate" them. And they did their work. They never fail. I knew I was healed, that I couldn't help being healed because God was faithful; and I almost lost interest in my symptoms, I was so certain of the truth. The drugs went — I didn't know for nineteen years after my healing what became of them. I thought maybe God would send an angel to take them away; and I was watching for him, but the first thing I knew they were gone. And that alone wouldn't have helped much, but something else was gone. The specific, irresistible, indescribable craving produced by demon power was gone. The hideous black bird of prey that croaked, "Nevermore," had flown, never to return. I had no more use for morphine and chloral than for rat poison — had no room for them or any other drugs in my physical economy. My appetite became so excellent that I had to eat about seven meals a day, and I had no room for drugs. And needless to say, my soul was filled with His praises: "My soul doth magnify the Lord, and my Spirit hath rejoiced in God my Saviour."

And the best of all is that this healing was no happy accident, no special miracle on my behalf but the working out in me of God's will for all of us — perfect soundness by faith in the Name of Jesus of Nazareth. So far as I know the field, God's work is being done today principally by men and women who have been raised from physical as well as spiritual death, people who were given up to die by the medical profession. I believe I could give offhand the names of one hundred such.

And there are still vacancies in the ranks of the army of the King. If you are afflicted, step out and receive healing and then get to work.

I was in Chicago immediately after my healing and went one day to the Women's Temple to the noon prayer meeting. I don't know how it is now, but it used to be a rallying place for Christian workers; they came from the Moody Bible Institute and many missions and churches. When I walked in I found the preacher talking of the awful snares in which people who trifle with narcotic drugs, including tobacco, get entangled. He warned them to give them up entirely if they were tampering with them. And then he sat down. I knew from experience that they couldn't give them up unless they took Jesus; and so, prompted by the Holy Spirit, I rose and asked if I might say a word. It was not parliamentary for me to do this, but God was in it, and I got leave. Then I said: "I am glad for the good advice our brother has given us and I want to tell you how to do it, and I am speaking from the depths of experience." And I told my story. I think many of them didn't believe in divine healing before I told it, but I don't believe there was one that didn't believe in it after I had finished. I was so happy, like some caged thing set free, that they couldn't help rejoicing with me; and spontaneously they rose to their feet and in one great burst of praise sang

> All hail the power of Jesus' Name
> Let angels prostrate fall,
> Bring forth the royal diadem,
> And crown Him Lord of all.

2

God's Will as Revealed in His Creative Work

"And God saw everything that he had made, and behold, it was very good" (Genesis 1:31).

I believe that one of the greatest hindrances to healing is the absence of certain, definite knowledge as to God's will. There is lurking in most of us a feeling that He may not be willing, that we have to persuade Him to heal us.

People often say, "I know that He is able; He has power if He only will" — like the leper in the eighth chapter of Matthew who said to Jesus, "If Thou wilt, Thou canst make me clean."

Many of us have been taught to pray, "If it be Thy will heal me." That wasn't the way David prayed: he cried in Psalm 6:2, "Have mercy upon me, O Lord, for I am weak: O Lord, heal me for my bones are vexed." He was evidently very ill indeed; and the excruciating pains in his bones might have been due to his extreme debility, for he goes on in the fourth and fifth verses imploring God to deliver him from impending death and then adds in the ninth verse, "The Lord hath heard my supplication; the Lord will receive my prayer."

There were no ifs nor buts in that prayer. The prophet Jeremiah too had no doubt about God's will as to healing, for he cried, "Heal me, O Lord, and I shall be healed; save me, and I shall be saved" (Jeremiah 17:14).

And we, God's people of this day, should be as free from doubt regarding our Father's will for our bodies as they were, for it is as clearly revealed in the Word as His will concerning the salvation of our souls.

In a sense the whole Bible is a revelation, not only of His willingness to heal our spiritual ailments, but our physical ones also. One of His covenant names is "the Lord that healeth" (Jehovah-rapha), and He is also the Lord that changeth not, the changeless, healing, health-bestowing, life-giving Lord, undisputed Sovereign over all the powers of the universe.

Jesus is the express image of the Father, the perfect expression of God and His Holy will. He could say, "He that hath seen me hath seen my Father also," and He declared that His works were not His own but the Father's that sent Him. He healed *all* who came to Him, never refusing a single individual. You cannot find a case where He said, "It is not My will to heal you," or "It is necessary for you to suffer for disciplinary purposes." His answer was always, "I will," and this fact forever settles for us God's will in regard to sickness.

Of course it has to be according to our faith, for faith is the hand that receives the gift, and God can only fill it to overflowing. I once offered a wee child some goodies, and I asked him to hold out his hands; and, oh, how sorry I was that they were so tiny. Let us pray God to enlarge our grasp of faith, for we are not straitened in Him, but in our own bowels, as the apostle puts it.

As the whole Bible is a revelation of God's willingness to heal and keep our bodies, as well as to save and keep our souls and spirits, we will start at the very beginning and ascertain what the first chapter of Genesis has to teach us about the matter.

There we find God's will clearly revealed in His creative work. God created man the way He wanted him, did He not? Did He make him with any disability or disease or tendency thereto? Was he deformed in any way? one leg shorter than the other, for instance? one shoulder higher than the other? or a squint in one eye?

No, we read that God said, "Let us make man in our image, and after our likeness" (Genesis 1:26). Wasn't that wonderful? Doesn't it thrill you? It ought to.

God had created many beautiful and wonderful things before this — the sun, the moon, the stars, noble trees, exquisitely beautiful plants and blossoms, sea monsters, fish and land animals, some of them of surpassing strength, others models of grace and beauty. But when it came to His masterpiece, man, He did not fashion him after any of these patterns; no, the model after which man was framed was a *divine* one. God said, "Let us make man in *our* image, after *our* likeness"; and after the work was done, God saw it and "behold it was very good."

Man then, prior to the fall, was in some sense in

the image of God, even as to his physical constitution; and there is no doubt that we have not at the present time any adequate idea of what a glorious being he was. Strong, beautiful, perfectly proportioned, magnificent, he stood forth a majestic and worthy head of creation.

Even to this day, though sadly defaced and marred by sin and its results, the human body bears the impress of the divine image and superscription as surely as the coin they handed to Jesus bore that of Caesar. I shall never forget the first time I saw a human brain. I was only a young girl, a medical student, worldly, utterly forgetful of my Creator in the days of my youth. But I can truly say that a feeling akin to holy awe filled me when I beheld it in all its wondrous complexity and beauty. Yes, those pearly gray, glistening convolutions seemed to me the most beautiful things I had ever seen. And when I realized that they were the home of thought parts of the organ through which the most intricate processes of reasoning were carried out, the marvel of it nearly stunned me. I could have fallen on my knees, young heathen though I was, before this mystery and its Author, the writing and superscription were so evidently divine.

In studying the anatomy of the human body, there are always two things that impress the careful observer. One is the perfection of the plan on which it is constructed down to the minutest cell: the marvelous adaptation of each part of the organism to its proper function, the wonderful cooperation between different organs and systems of organs, the perfect coordination of all the various parts and tissues to a common end.

The other thing that impresses one is the imperfections that meet you at every point. The trail of disease, or a tendency thereto, is over the whole organism, producing debility and sometimes structural changes resulting in deformity. Evidences of disease of some kind, hereditary or otherwise, are apparent upon close examination of almost any human body, though these are of course much more marked in some cases than others.

Yet while this is true, the plan of the whole and the marvelous manner in which it is carried out is so eloquent of infinite and divine wisdom that we instinctively take our shoes from off our feet and vail our faces as we reverently view God's handiwork.

A great scientist once said these words in commenting on the facts that I have just stated:

> I cannot understand how the consummate Artist who formed and painted a rose could also create a worm to gnaw at its fragrant heart, and cause its pink, flushed, velvet petals to turn the color of decay; neither can I understand how the Creator of such a glorious being as Man can bring into existence a foul and voracious thing like a cancer to prey upon that masterpiece of beauty and perfection, the human body.

No, apart from God's Word we are in Egyptian darkness regarding this problem of the ages, but the moment we accept the divine revelation it is as clear as noonday. God created man, the head of a new order of beings, perfect in spirit, soul, and body, free from all deformity and disease, a reflection of the beauty and glories of his Creator. "Whatsoever God doeth it shall be forever" (Ecclesiastes 3:14). So this is *His eternal purpose concerning us.*

The marring of God's masterpiece, man, in spirit, soul, and body, is the work of that malign being called Satan, which he effected by leading him to transgress God's law, thus introducing sin into the world with all its disastrous results.

Once a man gets out of line with God's will he is open to all sorts of satanic power which, entering him, defiles, deforms, and ultimately destroys every part of his threefold being. "The thief cometh not, but for to steal, and to kill, and to destroy: I am come that they might have life, and that they might have it more abundantly" (John 10:10).

But our refuge is in God and He will not fail us. His eternal purpose that we should be perfect as our heavenly Father is perfect, revealed in His creative work as well as being explicitly stated in the text of the Word, remains unchanged. He has made provision for its fulfillment in you and me; for Jesus Christ was manifested to destroy the works of the devil (1 John 3:8), whether sin, sickness, or death, so that we may be preserved blameless in spirit, soul, and *body* unto His glorious appearing. "Faithful is he that calleth you, who also will do it" (1 Thessalonians 5:24).

In closing let me quote a few words on this subject from Dr. F. W. Riale, who has received much illumination on the Word regarding our bodies:

> We are to reckon ourselves dead unto sin and alive unto God, and He will, as in the great faith of Abraham reckon this unto us in a most glorious righteousness. We are to feel that all sickness, like all sin, goes down forever in this great faith conflict. He forgiveth all our sins and healeth all our diseases.
>
> We are to cast all our diseases on the same Lord we cast all our sins upon. His Spirit coming in must banish all as far as the east is from the west. The

life of God in the soul of man must mean that the diseases of men go like the sins of men in the fire of the divine life and the divine love. . . . Believe in thy heart that God will most surely accomplish that which He has promised to those who believe, and thou shall be gloriously saved from all the disease that man falls heir to. . . . The Kingdom of Heaven, where sin and sickness are doomed and downed forever, is at hand. It is *now*. Only believe this and thou wilt see the glory of God in thy life.

3

The Source of Sickness

One fine morning I was called by telegram to a certain rural settlement — a beautiful and very rich farming district — where I found a terrible state of affairs. A number of people, including some of their very finest young men, were smitten by an awful scourge, a malignant type of typhoid fever. One magnificent specimen of young manhood, a boy of about seventeen, perfectly proportioned, with an intellectual head and a noble face, the oldest son of his father who was one of the wealthiest men in the vicinity, was in the article of death — perfectly unconscious — when I arrived.

Needless to say I did what I could, ministered to the sick ones according to the best methods then in vogue, but do you think I stopped with that?

You know I did not. I should have been guilty of criminal negligence if I had not taken steps to have the source of the infection discovered, with the view of shutting it off absolutely and so stamping out the deadly disease.

And the last time I visited that beautiful place I found a great change. The farmers had completely altered their manner of life. The water supply was now free from taint; and the most sanitary methods prevailed in their homes, stables, and dairies so that their connection with the source of the epidemic was shut off; and I never heard of any more typhoid fever in that district. I don't think they ever had any more.

Do you understand the parable? I am sure you do. We have learned from our study of God's creative work that it is His will that His masterpiece, man, should be — as He was created — in the image of God. "Very good," free from all deformity, disability, and disease. This is God's eternal purpose regarding man, for whatsoever "God doeth it shall be forever" (Ecclesiastes 3:14). That being the case, let us ask what is the source of all the disease that we see about us, that is working in some of our homes and even in our bodies.

And let us make the enquiry with the view of shutting off our connection with the source of the evil, if it be possible, so that we may stand perfect and complete in all the will of God as it is revealed in His Word, our "whole spirit and soul and body . . . preserved blameless unto the coming of our Lord Jesus Christ" (1 Thessalonians 5:23).

It was the best thing that ever happened to those farmers when they discovered that the typhoid was due to dead hogs in the water supply, for they could get rid of them and keep rid of them for all time to come. If they had gone on drinking dead hog soup, they would have gone on having typhoid; but they didn't have to go on drinking it, for there was plenty of pure, sparkling water, free from all germs, to be had for the taking. And I believe that God will enable me to point out something important from His Word to all who will listen in faith. First, the source of sickness, and second, how it may be absolutely shut off and how we may drink of the water of life freely, instead of the contaminated wells of earth (which like the water supply in the typhoid infested district, contain the water of death).

Let us go back then to the book of Genesis, and we shall find Satan, the source of sin and sickness, making his initial attack on man in the words addressed to Eve: "Yea, hath God said?" (Genesis 3:1).

Satan was compelled to attack God's Word, to question the authenticity of the divine revelation; for so long as man rests on the Word of God, he is perfectly invincible, impregnable, immovable. "They that trust in the Lord are like Mount Zion, which cannot be removed, but abideth forever" (Psalm 125:1).

Satan cannot touch them, rather they are the most serious menace to all satanic devices, plans, plots, and schemes, for to them has been given power over all the power of the enemy.

There is not a reinforcement which the prince of darkness can order up from the profoundest depths of his dark domain for which those who believe God's Word are not more than a match; not a poison gas manufactured in hell which the Breath of God will not dissipate; not a fiery dart which the shield of faith will not quench; not a pestilence which the precious Blood, boldly displayed on the lintel and doorposts of our dwellings, will not avert.

"No weapon that is formed against thee shall prosper" (Isaiah 54:17). So whether it be shot, or shell, gas, liquid fire, bombs, tanks, submarines, airplanes, artillery, cavalry or infantry, pestilence, famine, earthquake, lightning, or malicious tongues, we are perfectly safe so long as we are abiding in the Word of God.

Satan must dislodge us from our refuge in the secret place of the Most High before he can so much as touch us. Hence his introductory remark to our mother Eve: "Yea" — he always propitiates, conciliates, agrees with us as much as possible, avoids antagonizing us unnecessarily — "Yea, hath God said?"

> "Hath God said!" was hatched in hell,
>   Hear the serpent speak that word.
> Every soul that ever fell
>   Entertained that thought of God.
> God hath said; Yes, God hath said.
>
> God hath said; Yes, search the Word,
>   For what God hath said is all —
> All you need and more and more;
>   Here is most abundant store —
> God hath said; Yes, God hath said.
>
> God hath said, Lo! It is done.
>   What remains for us but praise?
> While He conquers in the fight,
>   Praise the Holiest in the height.
> God hath said; Yes, God hath said."

Yes, "God who at sundry times and in divers manners spake in time past unto the fathers by the prophets hath in these last days spoken unto us by His Son" (Hebrews 1:1, 2).

God hath said, and here in the Bible is what He said; and if we will but abide in that Word and treat any suggestion that would cast even the remotest doubt on the authenticity of this revelation or its living truth in every part of it to us at this moment as from the author of lies, continuous victory is ours.

My sister had a fearful physical test some time ago. For hours she coughed almost continuously. I have never heard anyone cough as she did. It was nerve-racking to hear her and constitution-racking to her to do it. She coughed till the whites of her eyes were scarlet from extravasated blood. Her cough was so violent that you would think she would burst in her effort to get her breath. I was kneeling beside her bed in the small hours of the morning taking victory. I reviewed the whole situation in the light of God's Word. Under that illumination I saw clearly that victory was hers. I took it, as it were, from the hands of God.

It seemed a concrete thing, round in shape and smooth to feel. The rotundity denoted, no doubt, the completeness of our redemption in Christ Jesus; the smoothness, the gentleness of God in all His dealings with us. It was pleasant to the touch. I knew that if she would take it into her hands and hold it there, Satan would flee and that she would breathe as deeply, quietly, and easily as ever in her life.

I so pressed it upon her by prayer and exhortation that twice she took it and held it lightly; but no sooner did she do this than Satan came as a roaring lion and bellowed in her very face; and in her fear, caused by the agonizing sense of suffocation which the enemy was allowed to put upon her, she let it slip from her nerveless grasp and was at his mercy — and he has none.

The Lord gave her the verse, "Your adversary the devil, as a roaring lion, walketh about, seeking whom he may devour; whom resist, steadfast in the faith"

(1 Peter 5:8, 9); for he may not devour those who rest on God's Word. If we resist the devil, James tells us, he will flee from us. So if he roars, you resist steadfast in faith in the Word. If he roars more, resist him more. If he keeps on roaring, keep on resisting. The louder he roars, the more vigorously you are to resist, and you will have the joy of seeing him flee before you as she did.

But, alas! Eve did not resist but allowed Satan to instill doubt which matured into unbelief and developed into disobedience; and sin, sickness, sorrow, and death entered into the world.

Then God gave them the promise of a Saviour and responded to the faith in that promise by bestowing on them redemption in type. He clothed them with garments not made by themselves, which cost the lives of innocent victims. These were placed on them by God's own hands and enveloped them, spirit, soul, and *body* in a covering of *blood.*

Here we have a beautiful picture of the redemption which is ours in Christ Jesus. Note that it takes in the body. God clothed them and enveloped their physical beings, as well as their souls and spirits, in a righteousness provided by sacrifice.

Jesus took the death penalty, which we had earned, and gave us His life, eternal life, instead. Hence, apprehension of Jesus Christ in all His offices by simple faith brings perfect peace; and thank God! " 'Tis everlasting peace, sure as Jehovah's throne."

But do you say, "I don't understand how the death of an innocent victim on my behalf can bring me peace"? No, we don't understand, that is true; but fortunately, we don't need to understand but only to believe, and that we can do.

This much we know because God tells us so in His Word, that under His holy law, which will never be altered or diminished in its requirements by so much as a jot or tittle, "the wages of sin is death." That death is not only the disintegration and ultimate dissolution of the body by the processes which we call disease or decay but also the separation of the spirit from God; it is something we have justly earned. And God must pay us our wages. Must do so, I say, in conformity with the constitution of His being, which is in its very essence, righteousness and holiness. If I am sovereign of the realm under an absolute form of government and I owe you certain wages and emoluments, I must in common justice pay them. On the other hand, if — under the constitution of the realm — I owe you the death penalty, I must inflict it or cease to be just and right before men and the tribunal of my own conscience.

God owes us something, and that something is death; and He must pay the debt. He will pay it in full — "the soul that sinneth, it *shall die*"! But Jesus Christ, who had no sin laid to His charge, ran in between the human race and the death penalty and bore it for us so that God, having made His Son suffer the full penalty for sin, can justly pardon us.

Now He only requires of us that we acquiesce in this wonderful plan of redemption, that we let ourselves be clothed. Don't come all dressed up in filthy rags of self-righteousness, but be arrayed, body, soul, and spirit in the righteousness (rightness) of Christ. This is divine healing and divine health. Never forget that it comes only through the shed Blood.

This teaching is not popular at present; but — what

matters a great deal more — it is true, for it is based on God's Word.

A great English artist was once seized with a divine hunger for a clearer vision of the Christ. He said, "If I could see Him in His beauty I could paint Him and make others see Him too." He thought if he could live where Jesus lived while on earth, breathe the same air, look on the same stars that shone upon the Holy One, he might get the vision. So he left everything — friends, home, fellow artists, studios, the applause of the multitude — and lived for years in a tiny tent in the awful solitudes that surround the Dead Sea. He was, like Paul, in peril of robbers, but nothing daunted him as day after day he turned the pages of his Bible. At last the Holy Spirit brought to him the words, "The Lord hath laid upon him the iniquity of us all," and he caught up his brush to paint the crucifixion, the spotless Lamb of God nailed to the tree. No, he could not touch brush to canvass; it seemed to sacred. He turned to the types and shadows of the Sacrifice — the high priest robed in garments of glory and beauty, the great Day of Atonement, the priest entering the holiest of all, not without blood, the people outside prostrate on the pavement. No, that was not it.

Again he turned to his Bible and a figure starts out from amidst the shadows, the figure of the scapegoat. It is led forward, and the sins of the people are confessed and laid upon it; the scarlet fillet is tied around its neck ("though your sins be as scarlet"). And as the doomed beast beneath its crushing load of guilt is led forth to the wilderness, the high priest turns to the people with words of absolution and comfort, "Ye are clean." And they return to their homes to enjoy the Sabbath rest, free from condemnation and doom; for it is God who has freed them from the burden of sin. But the doomed beast goes its lonely way far from the haunts of men. The moment chosen by the artist for his picture is the sunset hour. The animal is very near its end. Its strength is spent. The white lime soil is blood-marked from its wounded feet. It is crushed beneath its invisible load. Dying of starvation, parched with thirst, tottering with feebleness, eyes glazing, in its dumb distress it bears the curse that the guilty Israelites may go free and rejoice in his glorious liberty. This is a very faint picture of what this great redemption for spirit, soul, and body cost the Lord Jesus Christ. Surely we are bought with a price; therefore let us glorify God in our bodies and in our spirits, which are His.

Art critics were much disappointed in the picture, for the offense of the Cross has not ceased. But while it is foolishness to them that perish, to us who believe the cross of Christ is the power of God unto salvation, our only hope and plea, our sole glory.

And in that crushing load our sicknesses, as well as our sins, were borne; and not only that, but the Cross cast into the bitter waters of life, as at Marah, makes them sweet; and we need no longer drink of poisoned springs, for the Lamb will lead us to fountains of living waters.

So we can get rid of sickness and stay rid of it through the law of the Spirit of life in Christ Jesus:

> Banished my sickness, those Stripes did heal,
>   Because the work on Calvary is finished;
> Now in my body His life I feel,
>   Because the work on Calvary is finished.

4

Safety First

Let us go back in thought to the time when the children of Israel were in bondage in the wonderful old land of Egypt. For truly it was a wonderful land, a mighty empire, a surpassing civilization. It is an interesting fact that we really knew very little about that civilization until the beginning of the nineteenth century. Until then the most learned men in the world had utterly failed in their strenuous efforts to read the elaborate system of Egyptian hieroglyphics (the writing of the priests, a sort of sign language).

So we had nothing to go on regarding Egypt except the comparatively meager information in the Bible and the statements of Grecian historians; and the latter cannot be depended upon very much, for the writers themselves did not understand the ancient Egyptians.

But in the year 1799, a French officer discovered at a place in Egypt called Rosetta, a stone, called from the locality where it was found, the "Rosetta Stone." It contains inscriptions in Egyptian hieroglyphics, Greek, and demotic, the language of the Egyptian common people. It was soon discovered that the Greek was a translation of the hieroglyphics and also of the demotic, so the mystery was a mystery no longer.

When it became known that the Egyptian hieroglyphics had been deciphered, interest in everything Egyptian was greatly stimulated. Money was poured out like water for excavation and exploration in Egypt, and the country was filled with people bent on unraveling the long and jealously guarded secrets of the land of the Sphinx and the pyramids. And the results obtained have well repaid the expenditure of money and energy. For it was a wonderful land.

Even now all the great nations of the world have in their official museums, collections of Egyptian articles, books, furniture, works of art, tools, ladies' toilet articles, and yes, they had them even way back in the times of the Pharaohs and Ptolemies — games and toys. We know of their religion, with its elaborate ritualistic worship, and their Bible, called most appropriately, "The Book of the Dead." We have also learned that four thousand years before Christ they believed in the resurrection of the body and expended tremendous sums in mummifying human bodies because they expected the souls to rejoin them some day.

For my part, I shouldn't want the finest mummy that was ever mummified for a resurrection body. Should you? No. I want one made like unto His glorious body.

The Egyptians must have been engineers of outstanding skill, for I am a witness to the difficulty the best engineers in America encountered in removing the obelisk, which had been brought by ship from Alexandria, Egypt, from the dock to Central Park where it now stands. It is an immense thing, and it certainly made very slow progress along the narrow streets of lower New York.

Now why am I writing so much about Egypt? Why lay such emphasis on its wonders? Simply to bring out clearly that with all its wisdom, learning, glory, and beauty, God had but one use for Egypt so far as His children were concerned: and that was to get them out of it. "I loved him and called my son out of Egypt" (Hosea 11:1).

Egypt is a type of the world and it is a wonderful old world. It has all sorts of ingenious and beautiful things in it, but, like Egypt, it is one vast tomb; its Bible is a "Book of the Dead," for all who belong to it are dead in trespasses and sins. And so far as we are concerned, there is only one thing for us to do: and that is to come out of it — "Come out from among them and be ye separate . . . touch not the unclean thing" (2 Corinthians 6:17).

In the chapters of Exodus preceding the 11th, we find that God has been dealing with the Egyptians by means of awful judgments to make them let His people go, but all in vain. The heart of Pharaoh is obdurate, and God has come to the end of His long-suffering; and the final, awful judgment, the destruction of all the firstborn of Egypt by means of a pestilence unheard of in virulence and fatality, is impending.

In the first verse of the 11th chapter of Exodus, we find the Lord saying to Moses, "Yet will I bring one plague more upon Pharaoh and upon Egypt." These terrible words signed the death warrant of

Egypt's firstborn, chief of all their strength. "And Moses said, Thus saith the Lord, About midnight will I go out into the midst of Egypt and all the firstborn of the land of Egypt shall die, from the firstborn of Pharaoh that sitteth upon his throne, even to the firstborn of the maidservant that is behind the mill . . . And there shall be a great cry throughout all the land of Egypt, such as there was none like it, nor shall be like it any more" (Exodus 11:4-6).

This was to be the final plague, death in every house. Truly it was a terrible epidemic!

"But against any of the children of Israel shall not a dog move his tongue, against man or beast: that ye may know that the Lord doth put a difference between the Egyptians and Israel" (Exodus 11:7).

The Lord puts a difference between His people and those who are strangers to Him, as were the Egyptians; and the difference is the difference between life and death.

He draws a line, on one side of which is life — life more abundant, life for spirit, soul and body; and on the other side of which is death — death for spirit, soul, and body, the second death.

The Egyptians may have been as fair or fairer than the descendants of the Israelites. They may have been as good, from a human standpoint, or better than the offspring of Jacob; nevertheless, throughout the length and breadth of Egypt, from the king on his throne to the menial behind the mill, there was nothing but death. But in the dwellings of the Israelites there was peace and security and the sound of those who kept a holy solemnity unto the Lord as they feasted on the Passover Lamb.

What made the difference? What did the Israelites have that the Egyptians lacked?

Note that before God's clock struck the hour of doom there was a pause during which absolute safety, perfect immunity from disease and death was provided for all who would avail themselves of it — Israelites and Gentiles too; for there was a "mixed multitude" that went out with the children of Israel by the institution of the Passover, a type of the atoning work of Jesus Christ, the Sacrifice of the spotless Lamb of God.

Further, note that there was one, and only one, protection against this death-dealing epidemic, and that was the *blood*. The one thing that the Israelites had that the Egyptians lacked was the *blood* upon their dwellings.

The firstborn of Israel, as well as those of the Egyptians, were secure only through the *blood*. "When I see the *blood* I will pass over you, and the plague shall not be upon you" (Exodus 12:13).

All that the Egyptian physician could do — and they could do a great deal — was in vain. The history of medicine shows us that they had a most elaborate system of medicine and surgery. In an ancient graveyard dating back to 1500 B.C., skeletons were exhumed on which all sorts of delicate and difficult surgical work had been performed; and from the Ebers papyrus it is evident that the ancient Egyptians prior to and contemporaneous with Moses performed many surgical operations, including the removal of tumors and operations on the eye — in which department of surgery they were particularly well versed. Skulls on which trephining has been performed have been unearthed dating back as far as 2800 B.C.

Egyptian surgeons, who were also the priests and undertakers, were so skillful in their manipulation of the dead body that they removed the entire brain through the nasal orifices after death, in connection with the process of embalming. In this way they could avoid making the least change in the contour of the face which might have been occasioned if an incision had been made.

As to medicine, they had an extensive pharmaco-poeia, including castor oil and opium. They also used inhalations, potions, snuffs, fumigations, salves, cly-sters, injections, and poultices. They also seem to have had some quack medicines, or something very like them; for we read of a famous powder called "The Powder of the Three Great Men," while another bore the title, "Powder Recommended by Five Great Physicians." They were enthusiastic about elimina-tion and fasting in the treatment of disease, just as many doctors are today; and they had meat in-spected and water boiled if they thought them im-pure.

Yes, the physicians and surgeons of Egypt were doubtless capable and clever; but confronted with the deadly plague which slew the firstborn of Egypt, they were as helpless as infants. No doubt a consul-tation of the best medical men in the empire was hurriedly called by the royal physician whose business it was to watch over the health of the heir to the throne; but before they could assemble, he had passed forever beyond their reach. A gasp, a gurgle, a con-vulsive struggle for breath, bulging eyes, a livid hue about the lips, a stiffening of the muscles in the death agony, and the lineal descendant of all the Pharaohs was as dead as the son of the poor servant behind the mill.

Medical science is strictly limited in its possibilities and the best doctors are the first to confess this. The list of incurable diseases is long, very long, and even in the case of diseases that are classed as curable, the result of treatment is often palliative rather than curative. One of America's foremost physicians, now dead, said, "Back of all disease lies a cause which no remedy can reach."

The cause, we know from the Word of God, is sin; and for sin and its outworkings in the body in disease, debility, and deformity, there is but one remedy. And that remedy is the *blood of Jesus Christ, the Lamb of God.*

To this all efficacious remedy, and to it alone, the Israelites owed their immunity at the time of the awful visitation in Egypt. And, thank God! it has never lost its power.

During the epidemic of Spanish influenza — which baffled our modern physicians almost as much as the plague which destroyed the firstborn of Egypt baffled those of ancient Egypt — thousands of God's people were rendered perfectly immune by getting under the shelter of the Blood and staying there.

When the fell destroyer was literally raging in the town in which we lived, my sister said — by faith in the power of the Blood to all with whom she came into contact — "Here is one house on which you will never see an influenza placard; for the Blood is here, and God will not see it dishonored." And God made her boast in the Lord good; and though we were freely exposed to the disease (I myself never refusing to minister to the afflicted ones), our whole family enjoyed perfect immunity from it.

It was to the blood then, and to the blood alone, that the Israelites were indebted for their deliverance. Carefully note these four essential points with regard to the blood:

1. It had to be *shed*. The lamb must be slain. "Without shedding of blood is no remission" (Hebrews 9:22). "I determined to know nothing among you, save Jesus Christ, and him crucified" (1 Corinthians 2:2).

2. The blood had to be applied. "Through faith in his blood" (Romans 3:25).

3. The blood had to be applied *openly*. "Lintel and door post," in other words, a public confession of Christ crucified.

4. The blood had to be continually upon them. "Ye shall strike the lintel and the two side posts with the blood . . . and none of you shall go out at the door of his house until the morning" (Exodus 12:22).

The whole man — spirit, soul, and body — was thus continually sheltered behind the blood. So we must ever abide under the shadow of the Cross, and the result will be perfect physical, as well as spiritual victory.

The lesson which we are learning from the book of Exodus is that there is no safety apart from the Blood. Would to God that this truth might be burned into our very souls in these days of awful apostasy! So we might cry to those who are prating of "safety" while denying the Blood that bought them. "There is no safety except on the bleeding side of the Man of Calvary." We should shun as we would vipers all the literature put out by modernists so-called (they are as ancient as the devil himself), or the cults that trample under foot the blood of the Son of God; shed for our redemption if we would really and truly put "Safety First."

The end of this thrilling story we have been reading in Exodus is found in the following words from Psalm 105:37: "He brought them forth . . . and there was not one feeble person among all their tribes."

What a refreshing sight, a mighty nation, including thousands of aged men and women, tiny children and young mothers, and not one feeble among them all. Every frame erect and stalwart, every skin clear, every eye bright and shining, every man, woman, and child fit for the day's march — their strength as their day.

No wonder the fear and dread of them fell upon the surrounding nations and peoples as they marched along! No wonder Balaam had to confess "God is with him . . . he hath as it were the strength of an unicorn" (Numbers 23:21-22).

We are told that the things that happened to them were for an ensample unto us. God has provided "some better thing for us." They dwelt in types and shadows while we have the substance. Theirs were half lights while we have the full radiance of the outpoured Holy Spirit, who is come to lead us into all truth, to teach us all things. But what kind of a battlefront do we present as compared to theirs?

We are passing in procession down the aisles of the ages as truly as they did; we are being reviewed by a mighty host of witnesses including the heroes of faith of previous dispensations. Does not the thought come to you at times that we present but a sorry spectacle as compared to the Israelites? How many of us are limping along while others actually have to be carried on stretchers? What is the matter with us? Have we one promise less than they? Does not every assurance of physical health and healing which was made to them apply equally to us?

No one who believes the Word of God can answer this question other than affirmatively. God says, "I am the Lord that healeth thee"; "My word shall be health to all your flesh." And He also said, "I am the Lord. I change not."

The covenant of healing given them (Exodus 15: 26), which secured to them absolute immunity from disease, conditioned upon their obedience to God's statutes, is ours; and the condition need not frighten us, for by the obedience of One many are made righteous. And Christ is the end of the law for righteousness to every one that believeth, and the righteousness of the law is fulfilled in us who walk not after the flesh but after the Spirit. Therefore, not healing only, but absolute immunity from disease is ours in Christ Jesus as we walk in the obedience of faith.

That is what the world is looking for today. Chinese families are said to pay their doctors to keep them well, and the income of the family doctor ceases from that particular family if any one in the house becomes sick.

Western medical science is involved in the field of preventive medicine also, and I do not desire to belittle anything that may have been accomplished. But this I do say, that immunity from disease which is the dream, the unrealized ideal of medical science, is realizable by any simple child of God who will take his stand on the promises of God and not stagger at them through unbelief.

God wants us to be living epistles. This word is to be written in our very flesh in a language that all can read, for "He is the health of our countenance" (Psalm 42:11). And the heathen will have to say, "The Lord hath done great things for them" (Psalm 126:2), and they will seek the Lord our God.

5

A Wonderful Tree

"The Lord showed him a tree" (Exodus 15:25).

The last chapter dealt with the institution of the Passover and of the triumphant march of the Israelites out of the Egyptian bondage under which they had groaned for upwards of 400 years. These events are absolutely without parallel in history, whether sacred or profane. With a high hand, an outstretched arm, and mighty signs and wonders, God delivered them; and they made their exit from the land of the Pharaohs where they had been so long in thraldom, laden down with the treasures of their former masters. For we read in Exodus 12:35 that, according to the word of Moses, they "borrowed" from the Egyptians jewels of gold and silver, as well as raiment.

I once heard a learned Jewish convert to Christianity tell an incident in relation to this text which I have found most instructive to illustrate how people, who know nothing about it, will venture to criticize the Word of God.

He had dropped into a meeting of socialists in a hall in London, England, just as a speaker was saying: "The God of the Christians! The God of the Christians is a thief, a robber. In the 12th chapter of Exodus, we read that he directed the Israelites on their departure from Egypt to 'borrow' jewels of silver, jewels of gold and raiment, which they could never return. And they obeyed Him and spoiled the Egyptians."

The Jewish convert rose and asked to speak, and when the request was granted, he said: "I think, my friend, that you should know something more about the Bible and its Author, God, before you undertake to criticize it. I am a Hebrew; that Book is written in my mother tongue. The word in the original is not 'borrow' but 'ask' (that is the marginal reading in the Bible), and the real meaning of the word is *demand*. Surely you who profess to be so anxious to see all men righteously dealt with, ought to be the last to object to this. Demand recompense for all your centuries of toil, for your labor, your sweat, your blood, the lives which the cruel lash of the slave master have cost. And this is what they did."

Well, to resume the wonderful tale, the Children of Israel were led out and, by God's itinerary, brought to the Red Sea at a point where they were walled in by perpendicular rocks while the horses and chariots of Pharaoh were heard in full pursuit in the rear. At God's command they marched forward, and the Red Sea which also heard His voice, promptly piled itself up on either side so that they passed dryshod between colossal walls of water. They reached the other side and held a jubilee of triumph. Miriam led in the dance as the maidens played on the timbrels.

> Sound the loud timbrel o'er Egypt's dark sea,
> Jehovah hath triumphed, His people are free.

But alas! alas! alas! the echo of these strains of joy have hardly died away before they are replaced by murmuring against God. Can it be possible? Only a short time since these people were doubtless saying: "For my part, after what I have seen with my own eyes and heard with my own ears, I shall never forget the wonder of it! I can never doubt again."

No, not until the next time. Here we find them in Exodus 15:23 murmuring because the waters at Marah were bitter. You would think they would have reflected that the God who had delivered them, who had rolled back the Red Sea at their cry, could also remedy this trouble; but no, they murmured against Moses. When people are not right with God and want to murmur but are afraid to find fault with Him, they are apt to attack His servants. So let us be careful if we find that tendency in our hearts even — much less bitter words on our lips. They had forgotten that it is through our needs that God reveals Himself to us.

Jehovah is distinctively the redemption name of God; and in His redemptive relation to man, Jehovah has seven compound names which reveal Him as meeting fully every need of man from his lost estate to the glorious ending of a completed redemption. Physical healing can be clearly seen in each of the seven.

1. *Jehovah-Jireh.* "The Lord will provide" (Genesis 22:8). Our first need was a perfect Sacrifice, and that God provided by giving His Son, the spotless Lamb of God, to bear our sins *and sicknesses* on that cruel tree on the hill of the Skull near Jerusalem.

2. *Jehovah-rapha.* "The Lord that healeth" (Exodus 15:26).

3. *Jehovah-nissi.* "The Lord our banner" (Exodus 17:8-15); The Lord who fights our battles for us when Satan would attack us whether in soul or body.

4. *Jehovah-Shalom.* "The Lord, our peace" (Judges 6:24). Only one who is in perfect health, physically as well as spiritually and mentally, can be kept in perfect peace; and Jesus offers Himself to us as peace for our triune beings, for "He is our peace" (Ephesians 2:14).

5. *Jehovah-ra-ah.* "The Lord our shepherd" (Psalm 23:1). The physical well-being of the sheep is the shepherd's responsibility. He applies the healing balm from his horn of oil to the sores and bruises. So Jesus the Good Shepherd heals those who are His.

6. *Jehovah-tsidkenu.* "The Lord our righteousness" (Jeremiah 23:6). Righteousness, or "rightness" for spirit, soul, and body, all three of which God teaches us to pray may be preserved blameless unto the coming of our Lord Jesus Christ.

7. *Jehovah-shammah.* "The Lord is present" (Ezekiel 48:35). The same Jesus who healed all who were oppressed by the devil is with us today.

The bitter waters of Marah reminds us that life, of which water is a type as it forms the great bulk of all living things, is embittered at its very fountain head. The tiny baby is hardly born into the world before the anxious mother is enquiring whether it is strong, or if it shows any evidence of this or that hereditary disease, or any tendency thereto; and the saddest thing of all is that every baby has some inherited morbid predisposition, if not an actual disease, when it arrives in this sphere.

And when the Israelites were brought face to face with the bitter waters of Marah, God was there to reveal Himself to them under a new name to meet the new need: "The Lord that healeth" [present tense, that always heals — present, continuous healing].

And the Lord showed Moses *a tree!* Oh, for a fresh, God-given vision of that *tree* and the fruit that it bears! Truly as it is put in the Song of Solomon, we can sit down under its shadow with great delight, and its fruit is sweet to our taste.

There is a substance known in chemistry that is about 700 times sweeter than sugar. It was discovered accidentally by a chemist when he was experimenting with coal-tar products. He had been called to dinner, and after washing his hands in the laboratory as usual, changed his coat and sat down at the table. Taking a sip of tea, he was disgusted to find it sweeter than the sweetest syrup he had ever tasted. He was about to remonstrate with his wife but took a bite of bread first to take the cloying taste of the sweetness out of his mouth. To his amazement, the bread tasted like the richest cake. The thought occurred to him, "Is it possible that *I* am sweet?" He put his thumb in his mouth to suck it like a baby, and it was as though he had a sugar plum in his mouth. To his wife's surprise he jumped and ran to the laboratory where he carefully examined the contents of every test tube and crucible. At last he found the compound he had accidentally produced when boiling some chemicals together, the vapor from which had gotten into his throat, on his lips, and into his lungs, so that he was all sweetness.

When we see this *tree* in the light which the Holy

Ghost sheds upon it through the Word, everything becomes sweet:

> Never further than Thy cross,
>   Never higher than Thy feet;
> There earth's richest things are dross,
>   There, earth's bitterest things are sweet.

Yes, everything is sweet to us for we are ourselves sweet; nay, rather we are sweetness if Jesus, who is the Word of God and who is sweeter than honey and the honeycomb, is dwelling and reigning within us. For "it is no longer I, but Christ who dwelleth in me." That was a wonderful *tree* that God showed Moses, and it bears wonderful fruit.

When Jesus, Moses, and Elias met in the glory of the Mount of Transfiguration, there was no theme so fitting for their discourse as the decease which Jesus was to accomplish at Jerusalem. For that death was the greatest achievement that this world has ever witnessed, the only act of sacrifice acceptable to God that has been performed by a human being — for Jesus was true man as well as "very God of very God" — since the Fall. For all the righteous acts of the saints are necessarily performed in the power of that one sacrifice of Himself, by which He hath forever perfected them that are sanctified and are, as it were, an integral part of that accomplishment. On that *tree* we find pardon and peace, healing and health, victory over death and hell; for by His death on that *tree* Jesus conquered death and him that hath the power of death. "Bowed to the grave, destroyed it so, and death, by dying, slew."

That *tree* was most fittingly set up on Calvary (Latin, *Calvarium,* the place of the skull), the very

zenith of Satan's power. For what more fully shows
the depth of man's fall than the transformation of
the beautiful human countenance, radiant with intelligence, and glowing with emotion, bearing the impress of the divine image upon its lineaments, into a
ghastly, grinning, gruesome skull?

This then is the tree that God showed Moses,
which, when cast into the waters, made them sweet.
In a book which I have been reading, it is stated that
the waters in the vicinity of Marah are still bitter from
excess of alkali salts but that the fount which was
healed by the branch can still be distinguished from
the others by its comparative sweetness. Notice, that
the *tree* had to be cast into the waters; that is, the
atoning merits of Christ have to be applied to our
own particular case of sin, sickness, or both as the
case may be, by our own personal faith.

I am told that in the public library at Boston,
Massachusetts, Sargent, one of the greatest of modern artists, has brought out most beautifully and clearly in his mural decoration, "The Dogma of Redemption," the truth of our deliverance from sin, sickness,
and death through the sacrifice of Christ.

In the picture, Jesus hangs on the cross, and on
either side of Him are our first parents, Adam and
Eve, each holding in their hands golden chalices in
which they are catching drops of the precious blc
which flows from His pierced hands. Above the cross
are the words, "Dying for the Sins of the World,"
and beneath the whole, the inscription, "He came to
redeem our bodies and to cleanse our hearts." In all
the work there is a strong line of demarcation between celestial and terrestrial, but the uplifted cross
breaks through this and lets heaven and earth run

into one. Praise God! That is what the cross does for us. The cross itself is upheld by angels whose faces are radiant with bliss as though they comprehended the final, fullest, most glorious purpose of God in the Supreme Sacrifice and could not contain their joy. And the instruments of agony, the scourge, the hammer, the spear are all held in the hands of angels who are bathed with the rest of the scene in unutterable glory.

May God in His mercy show us the *Tree,* and when we see it may we apply it to our hearts and lives, our spirits, souls, and bodies, so that we may become the very sweetness of Jesus. "There He made for them a statute and an ordinance, and there He proved them!"

The Word of God always proves or tests us. Some people say, "I will try God's promises for healing." No, you won't; they will try you. God's promises are tried, purified seven times, forever settled. *You* are the one that is on trial. God is not on trial. His truth reaches to the heavens and His faithfulness to the clouds. He made this statute and ordinance and they have never been repealed. He sealed them with His covenant, and forevermore He is Jehovah-rapha, the Lord that healeth. They are conditional upon our diligent hearkening and faithful obedience. But before He made these conditions He showed us the *Tree.*

That Tree cast into our lives will remove every trace of the bitterness of sin and rebellion from our natures and make us sweet with the heavenly sweetness of our Lord. Then we can claim absolute immunity from all the sickness which is brought by God in His righteous judgments on the Egyptians.

The great poet Dante has placed in his poem, "Inferno," over the portal of hell, the well-known words, "All hope abandon ye who enter here." But as we enter as little children into the kingdom of heaven through faith in a crucified Saviour, we read in golden letters, "All fear abandon, ye who enter here." For He hath redeemed us from all evil and will preserve us blameless in spirit, soul and body unto His glorious coming.

6

The Praise Cure

I have administered a good many cures, seen a
good many administered, and heard about a good
many more. I remember a friend of mine telling me
of one she took. But whatever the results might have
been, they were certainly not lasting, as she repeated
it every year; and she complained, moreover, that it
was very unpleasant.

"It was horribly expensive as well," she continued; "but as I had plenty of money in those days,
that didn't matter so much; but the unpleasantness of
it, I shall never forget."

"What was there so unpleasant about it?" I inquired.

"Well, to begin with I had to go to Austria for it,
for only there is a certain kind of mineral water to be
found, which my doctor says my constitution needs.
It is horribly nasty, tastes like sulphur matches and
rotten eggs would taste, to judge by the smell. When
I got there I was put in a little attic room and had to

be thankful to get it, the place was so crowded. It was a room such that I should not dare ask anyone in America to sleep in, not even a tramp. Then we were wakened in the morning at five o'clock by a sort of clapper which made a very loud and grating noise. At the very first stroke we had to leap up."

"Why such haste?"

"Because if we didn't get up immediately we should be late, and that meant no breakfast. That was part of the cure!"

"Oh, I understand. I suppose, then, you hastily took your bath and ran down to a well-prepared meal."

"That's all you know about it. There was no bath-room, and, already blue with cold, I had to wash in a hand basin in ice water. Honestly I have sometimes found a thin film of ice on the water in the jug. Then I had to dress as quickly as I could in all my outdoor things, including heavy walking boots, and put on a warm wrap. I then dashed downstairs to join the procession on the way to breakfast."

"Why, where was the breakfast?"

"Oh, miles and miles away. That was part of the cure. The road was very rough; I think that was part of the cure too, to shake up your liver."

"Well, I suppose you arrived at last and went into a building where they had a huge open fireplace with great logs burning in it and sat down in front of its grateful warmth to a substantial German breakfast, all steaming hot."

"That shows all you know about it. No, when we reached our destination, we were at a sort of fountain surrounded by a platform which was always slippery and damp, where we formed in line and at last reached the man who dispensed the water. When you gave your name, he turned to a file he had to see how many glasses you had to drink and handed them to you, one by one, watching to see that you consumed the last drop of each. Then, and not till then, he handed you a ticket that entitled you to breakfast; and you made a mad rush with the rest of the patients to a sort of garden, only it had no flowers in it, only some discouraged shrubs. Here there were some small tables (for we always took our meals in the open air if possible, that being part of the cure), on which were rolls of some kind of black bread; but I tell you it tasted good, and the only trouble was the rolls were so small."

"But you could eat plenty of them, I suppose," I interjected.

"Maybe you're a doctor, but it's plain to me that you know nothing about cures," my friend said almost contemptuously. "No, we were allowed only two rolls at the most; some patients got only one all the time they were there. Once in a great while some of us got an egg each or a very thin slice of cold meat with our roll, but that was only by the doctor's *special* order. Then we had a cup of very weak coffee made with milk. It was hot and was the only warm thing we encountered from the time we got up until dinner time. They usually had some very thin soup for dinner and two kinds of vegetables — very small helpings — and some days a tiny, tiny bit of meat or fish. No dessert, excepting on gala days, an apple. Supper wasn't worth mentioning, and often I was deprived of it altogether. This ordeal was considered a great cure and you had to apply months beforehand to be sure of getting in; and counting your traveling expenses, doctors' bills and board, it came very high."

That's one kind of a cure, and there have been and are many others; as the grape cure, where patients are allowed to eat all the ripe grapes they can get but nothing else of any kind; the barefoot cure, where they go barefoot; the hot mud cure — no, they didn't have to eat it, only wallow in it. And I am far from saying that nothing is accomplished by these and other kindred methods, but I do say that the cure of which I am going to speak is the only sure cure. It is the most expensive one ever known, but the price was paid by another; for "it was purchased, not with corruptible things, as silver and gold . . . but with the precious blood of Christ, as of a lamb without blemish and without spot" (1 Peter 1:19). And the poorest may enjoy its fullest benefits. I call it the praise cure because it is most readily applied by simply singing yourself into it: "Enter into his gates with thanksgiving and into his courts with praise: be thankful unto him, and bless his name" (Psalm 100: 4). You know you can sing yourself and shout yourself into and through things that you can't get into or through in any other way.

There was an old Presbyterian elder who was terribly opposed to anybody making a noise over his religion. He thought religion should be like the newest style of typewriters, absolutely noiseless and with a guarantee to that effect. He had one daughter, however, a most saintly girl who had so much glory in her soul that she occasionally boiled over. He labored with her to no effect; for it seemed as though she could not help it, though she hated to grieve her old father. At last one day the old man came to the end of his well-spent life; and as he felt himself entering the valley of the shadow of death, he had a glimpse of the glory that is to be revealed. And to the amazement of all his family, he gave one shout of great joy and cried for his shouting girl, "Come along, daughter, and help me shout my way through clear home to glory." And that is exactly what she did, though the tears were streaming down her face all the while.

And we can stand on God's Word for salvation and healing after we have met God's conditions and grounded every weapon of rebellion. We can praise our way through to perfect manifested victory. This I call the praise cure, and it never fails when the praise is the outflow of a heart resting on God's unchanging Word.

There was a missionary to China staying at Mrs. Carrie Judd Montgomery's Beulah Heights in Oakland, California. She had the most wonderful healing of smallpox while on the field by the application of the praise cure.

She fearlessly nursed a sister missionary who had the disease though she had not been vaccinated, standing on God's promise that no plague should come nigh her dwelling. Then a very bad case of confluent smallpox — that was what it looked like to the doctors — came out on her and she did not know what to do; so she asked the Lord, and He told her to sing and praise Him for faithfulness to His word. They isolated her and told her to lie quiet, but she said if she didn't praise God the very stones would cry out. So she sang and sang and praised and praised. The doctor said he feared for her life, that the case was serious and awful complications threatened. But she praised and praised and sang and sang.

He said she was evidently delirious but that he had so little help that he couldn't restrain her — and she sang and sang and praised and praised. They told her that if by any chance she recovered, she would be disfigured for life — and she sang and praised louder than ever. They asked, "Why do you praise so much?" She answered, "Because I have so many pocks on me. God shows me I must praise Him for each one separately." And she kept right at it.

The Lord had shown her a vision of two baskets, one containing her praising — half full — and the other, in which was her testing — full. He told her that the praise basket must be filled so that it would out balance the other, so she kept at it. Her songs and shouts were so Spirit-filled that they were contagious, and the Christian nurses couldn't resist joining in; so they kept the place ringing. At last the Lord showed her that the praise basket was full and overflowing. She saw it sink and the testing basket rise in the air; and in a moment, as it seemed, the eruption and all attendant symptoms vanished, leaving no trace in the way of so much as a single scar.

Perhaps that may seem almost too much to believe to some, but I can furnish from my own personal experience a case where the smallpox eruption disappeared instantaneously in answer to believing prayer and the application of the praise cure.

One evening we were about to open the meeting at a mission where I was then working when a man rushed into the hall and asked to have a few moments of private conversation with me. After I led him to the prayer room, he said, "Dr. Yeomans, my wife has just broken out all over with smallpox!"

"How do you know that it is smallpox?" I inquired.

"Why, we had a doctor who said so and told us not to stir from the house as he was going down to get the health doctor and have the place quarantined without a moment's delay. But as soon as he had left the house, my wife said, 'Run down to the mission. Ask Dr. Yeomans to pray, and I am sure God will clear this plague off my skin and out of my blood.'"

So right on the spot we applied the praise cure, and the brother ran home to find his wife without a single trace of the disease. A little later the doctor returned with the health doctor and was unmercifully teased by the latter for reporting a case of smallpox when there wasn't a pock in sight, nor any symptom of disease.

"Where is your smallpox?" the health officer inquired.

"Well, where is it? It was here when I left."

"Well, where is it now?" inquired the health doctor; and with some jokes as to the probable character of the beverages which his colleague had been indulging in, he left the place without any further comment.

Yes, the praise cure works every time. It is not unpleasant; rather it is delightful; the cost of it has been met for us by another, and it is available this moment to each of us.

Are you ready to begin it? The last clause of 1 Peter 1:8 tells us exactly how to begin: *"Believing, ye rejoice with joy unspeakable and full of glory."*

Just believe what God says that Jesus has done for you, body, soul, and spirit — think about it, talk about it, sing about it, shout about it, and the praise cure has begun. You are not to take it once a year but all the time. "I will bless the Lord at all times: his praise shall continually be in my mouth" (Psalm 34:1). The Psalms — the book of praise inspired by the Holy Spirit, which has been used by the people of God in all ages and which Jesus Himself used — are full of this praise cure. Just observe the first verses of Psalm 103: "Bless the Lord, O my soul: and all that is within me, bless His holy name. Bless the Lord, O my soul, and forget not all his benefits: who forgiveth all thine iniquities; who healeth all thy diseases; who redeemeth thy life from destruction; who crowneth thee with lovingkindness and tender mercies; who satisfieth thy mouth with good things; so that thy youth is renewed like the eagle's."

I personally knew a man who was dying of acute tuberculosis of the lungs who praised himself into perfect, rugged health that lasted a lifetime. His remarkable recovery and good health was the result of following the words of this Psalm. Begin now. You can't afford to postpone it by so much as a moment. Tread the young lions under your feet by the praise of faith. It has never failed and never will.

Sometimes people say, "That's true and I feel better already. But when Jesus spoke the word when He was here in person, the symptoms always disappeared instantly; and mine haven't disappeared or have only partly disappeared; so I can't be healed."

The scriptural answer to this difficulty is that the symptoms did not always disappear immediately, even when Jesus was here in person.

The nobleman's son, referred to in John 4 "began to amend," get better, improve, convalesce, at the seventh hour, when the fever left him.

The healing of the blind man at Bethsaida, related in Mark 8, is not only markedly gradual but in three distinct, separate stages.

First, Jesus took him by the hand and led him out of Bethsaida, which city He had abandoned to judgment. (See Mark 8:23; Matt. 11:21-24.)

Second, Jesus began the healing with an anointing of spittle, after which He asked the man if he saw aught (anything). And the man replied that he saw men as trees walking; or, in other words, that he had a degree of distorted vision.

If the man who now possessed enough sight to enable him to blunder around had departed and told people that Jesus had healed him but that he could only see to get around and had no use of his eyes for work that required clear vision, I believe he would have done just what many thousands of people who come for prayer for healing are doing today. Those to whom he told his story would have said, "Well, that's the kind of work Jesus of Nazareth does, is it? It's a wonder He wouldn't have made a good job of it while He was at it." But that wouldn't have been Jesus' fault, would it? And it isn't His fault if you have not perfect soundness. If you are in the second stage, press through to the third one. For in it the man received perfect sight and saw every man clearly. Notice that Jesus made him look up (vs. 25), and that one look of faith to the Lamb of God brought perfect restoration of his sight. Let us look into His Face and praise Him for the fullness of the redemption He has purchased for us, for it is a wonderful cure — the praise cure — and the only unfailing one that has ever been discovered or ever will be discovered.

7

Timothy's Wine and Hezekiah's Poultice

"Drink no longer water [or "water only," marginal translation], but use a little wine for thy stomach's sake and thine often infirmities" (1 Timothy 5: 23). It is wonderful how many people can quote this verse more or less correctly. I remember hearing a preacher say that he had met those who couldn't quote another verse from the Bible but who were quite familiar with this one. I once had a seeker at the altar with whom I was dealing whose greatest weakness was a love for strong drink. He said, "But doesn't the Bible say that Timothy was told by the apostle Paul to use a little wine for his stomach's sake?"

"Yes, to be sure, Paul told Timothy to use a little wine for his stomach's sake, but that does not warrant you in using a *great deal* of whiskey to destroy your stomach, and all the rest of your organs," I replied.

And then I have had people quote it as their authority for using all sorts of drugs. Because Paul told Timothy to take a *little* wine, they felt clear to take a *great deal* of quinine or some laxative or favorite tonic or aspirin or Tanlac or other patent medicine.

Of course this matter is only part of a much larger question, namely, What is the attitude of the Word of God toward man-made systems of healing? But let us look into this question of Timothy's wine. In studying this passage, I do not feel free to omit what the eminent Bible scholar, Moffatt, says of this verse that it is "either a marginal gloss, or misplaced." But as it occurs in the King James and other versions in use among us, I shall consider it as belonging to the original text. I believe that in it Paul advised Timothy in regard to his diet, suggesting the substitution of the juice of the grape — which is most valuable from the standpoint of nutrition — for water as a beverage, just as though I should counsel one of you to take cocoa or other nourishing drink with your meals instead of water only. In the New Testament we are left perfectly free, under God, as to our diet. And so long as we eat and drink to His glory, we may consult our preferences as to the selection we make. Indeed, with a perfectly healthy person — and God makes us perfectly healthy if we trust Him — the tastes are an index of the requirements of the system and should be regarded as such. That God desires us to enjoy a variety of foods is evident from the fact that He has provided so many different kinds, each possessing some special property peculiar to itself and valuable to us. I believe that we should show our gratitude to Him; first by thanking Him for His lavish kindness in this regard; and second, by furnishing our tables with a varied diet, so far as our means will permit. There is no doubt that such a diet makes for health and efficiency. Children should be trained from their earliest days to eat and enjoy varied diet, comprising as many different kinds of vegetables and fruits as are obtainable, as well as nuts, a little meat, milk, eggs, butter, cheese, cereals, whole wheat bread, etc.

With reference to Hezekiah's poultice, we note from careful study that his case was a perfectly hopeless one. God Himself had told him to set his house in order, for he was going to die. The case has been analyzed by a distinguished Christian physician, author of a treatise on Bible diseases, and pronounced one of carbuncle, followed by general blood poisoning. A carbuncle is like a gigantic boil which involves the deeper tissues of the body. Hezekiah prayed and received God's promise of healing and was told that fifteen years would be added to his life. Isaiah then directed him to place a poultice of figs on the boil, but such an application could have no effect on the course of such a hopeless disease as carbuncle and general blood poisoning. It might have been used as a cleansing application. It used to be customary to cleanse ulcerating and discharging surfaces by applying large moist poultices of soft pultaceous material, such as bread and milk, linseed and charcoal, etc.; but they had no curative properties. On the other hand the order to place a lump of boiled figs on the boil or carbuncle may have been merely a test of Hezekiah's obedience, just as Naaman was ordered to dip seven times in Jordan. While on this point, allow me to quote the following from the *Sword of the Spirit*.

> Any means ever used in the Bible had no healing virtue in them whatever, and as we have already said in this article, were used only as a test of faith

and obedience. . . . When the children of Israel were bitten by the serpents in the wilderness, God told them the means by which they might be healed, which was for Moses to make a polished brass serpent and put it on a pole. One look at this serpent would bring pardon, cleansing, and healing to the bitten and dying Israelites. The serpent was preserved as a memorial of what God had done. A long time afterwards in Hezekiah's time, they began to depend on the virtue supposed to be in the serpent. This brought a stern rebuke from Hezekiah, who ground the serpent to pieces and threw it away.

Now let us consider the question referred to earlier in this chapter: What is the attitude of the Word of God toward man-made systems of healing?

Of the futility of turning to human physicians instead of to Him in sickness, God has given us three examples in the Bible. First, the illness and death of Ahaziah, king of Israel and son of Ahab, who enquired regarding his case of Baal-zebub, god of Ekron, instead of the Lord God of Israel (2 Kings 1: 2-4). Second, the illness and death of Asa who sought not the Lord but to the physicians, and "slept with his fathers" (2 Chronicles 16:12-13). I once talked with a doctor about different schools of medicine — allopaths, homeopaths, naturopaths, and others. He said, "*All* the 'paths' lead but to the grave, so it doesn't matter much which 'path' you take." That was where Asa's physicians led him, that is certain. And third, the woman who suffered many things of many physicians, spending all she had and was nothing better but rather grew worse (Mark 5:25, 26; Luke 8:43). It is worthy of note that Luke, himself a physician, does not speak of the woman having suffered many things of the medical fraternity and being rather worse than better as the result of their ministrations, though he mentions that she had spent all she had upon them. But the most striking thing about the attitude of the Word of God toward human systems of healing is that they are ignored therein as though they were nonexistent. In view of the fact that elaborate systems of medical science flourished during the periods covered by the Sacred Record, it seems that no words could be more eloquent than the divine silence regarding them.

The distinguished scientist, Dr. Albert T. Buck, in his exhaustive work on the history of medical science, after writing of the skill of ancient Egyptian physicians and surgeons, the many remedies including powders, inhalations, potions, snuffs, salves, fumigations, injections, etc., employed by them, their dietetic measures, eliminative treatment, and other therapies, adds a note about the Israelites. "The Israelites made small use of medicinal agents, dietetic measures and external applications. They placed their chief reliance on prayers, sacrifices and offerings."

No, the Israelites had no need for Egyptian remedies, efficacious though they may have been. Their God had promised that He would bring on them none of the diseases which He brought upon the Egyptians, for He is the Lord who heals His people. The history of medical science reveals the fact that from prehistoric times men have fought with all the powers of intellect they possess against sickness, but noble as have been their efforts — for science has its martyrs as well as religion, and many have actually laid down their lives in the battle against disease — they have yielded very unsatisfactory results, scientific men themselves being the witnesses. Note these words from the pen of H. A. Rowland, in the *American Journal of Science,* quoted by Dr. Fielding H. Garrison in his *History of Medicine.*

> An only child, a beloved wife, lies on a bed of sickness. The physician says the disease is mortal; a minute plant called a microbe has obtained entrance into the body and is growing at the expense of the tissues, forming deadly poisons in the blood or destroying some vital organ. The physician looks on without being able to do anything. Daily he comes and notes the failing strength of the patient; daily the patient goes downward until he rests in his grave. But why has the physician allowed this? Can we doubt that there is a remedy that will kill the microbe? Why then has he not used it? He is employed to cure but has failed. His bill we cheerfully pay because he has done his best and given a chance of cure. The reason for his failure to cure is ignorance. The remedy is yet unknown. The physician is waiting for others to discover it, or is perhaps experimenting in a crude and unscientific manner to find it.

And this sad confession is made after centuries and centuries of investigation, research, and effort, during which the animal, vegetable, and mineral kingdoms have literally been ransacked for remedial agents. In the 16th century A.D., a Chinese doctor published a work on medicine in 52 volumes, and at that time the Chinese had 1800 drugs in their regular pharmacopoeia.

Some people go so far as to say that medical science is God's way of healing His people, that He enables men to discover remedies in order that we may utilize them. If that were the case, Moses — who was versed in all the learning of the Egyptians, including medical science — would have so taught the children of Israel instead of pointing them always and only to God, the Lord, as their Physician. If medical science were God's chosen way of meeting our need in sickness, it would not be so uncertain, unreliable, fluctuating, and changing, nor so diverse in its teaching.

In all periods of the world there have been conflicting and rival schools of medicine as there are today. If the physician is God's way for me, I shall have to ascertain which physician, the regular, the homeopath, the eclectic, the osteopath, the chiropractor, the drugless, etc. No, God's way of healing is One, even Christ Jesus the Lord, who is not only the Way, but who is the Truth and the Life of spirit, soul, and body.

While we know that God always blesses men just as much as they will let Him bless them and meets them just where they are, we have the plain statement of the Scriptures that the Lord Himself is the Healer of His people, and His glory He will not give to another.

The great French physician, Charcot says, "The best inspirer of hope is the best physician." Our Physician is the God of hope, for the Lord Jesus Christ is Himself our Hope (1 Timothy 1:1). So in order to be true to God and His Word, it seems to me that we have to do as did His people of old and trust for our bodies, as well as our souls, to Him alone.

The Bible teaches that sin, sickness, and suffering actually exist, are real and not illusions of mortal mind as the Christian Scientists would have us believe. But it also teaches that they are completely removed by God in answer to believing prayer offered in the name of Jesus Christ, who Himself bore the full penalty of our sins in His body on the cross of Calvary. This truth, which was fully and simply accepted in apostolic times and for hundreds of years afterward, was later so mixed with prayers at the tombs of saints and the veneration of their relics, bones, clothing, and things of the kind, as to be almost lost to the church. But at the time of the Reformation it again came to light with the unearthing of the Scriptures and their diffusion among the people when many notable healings took place. With every subsequent revival the tide of divine healing has risen higher. Remarkable healings took place in the Quaker revival and the meetings led by the Wesleys, under Simpson, Dowie, Cullis of Boston, and others; and now in connection with the last great outpouring of the Holy Spirit, the mighty tide of healing is rolling in with an irresistable flood of blessing.

In this connection I shall quote some statements regarding a case of organic disease, tuberculosis of the lungs and spine, which was cured by the prayer of faith and anointing according to James 5:14. This healing came after all human means had been applied unsuccessfully, according to certificates furnished by the attending physicians, men eminent in the profession. The quotes are from the *Elim Evangel,* published in Belfast, Ireland, by Pentecostal leaders in Great Britain, among whom are Pastors George and Stephen Jeffreys.

Sister Edith Cuffley, the person who was healed, gave her testimony at a meeting at Elim Tabernacle, London.

I am led by God to let others know, especially those who are seeking Divine Healing, how very miraculously I was cured after being ill for four years and nine months. . . . I was a sewing-machine operator by trade, consequently my work was very heavy, especially so when the war broke out and I had to do soldiers' coats, tents, etc. . . . One day I collapsed while at work and had to be taken to the hospital. Two weeks later I had a very bad hemorrhage of the lungs and for two years I lay in my own home in Kennington, having a nurse daily to attend to me, and the doctor coming three times a week. During this time the doctor tried to get me into a hospital or sanatorium, but admission was not obtainable as by this time I had become a bedridden case; so then I began to lose all use of my limbs, and endured dreadful pain in my spine. The doctor found that the disease had traveled to the spine, and I was put under X-rays to make sure, and, to my great sorrow, it was found to be true. The pain became so great that my husband asked the doctor to try and get me away, and the only place that was available was the Home for Incurables and Dying, at Thames Ditton, where I lay from April, 1919, till August, 1920. Here my condition became very critical and a spinal jacket was made, with the hope that it might prove a support and enable me to sit up in bed. This, however, was quite useless, and when I was put into it the pain only increased. I got much worse, was put on a water bed, and given hypodermic injections, twice a day for eight months.

In August, 1920, she left the hospital in an apparently dying condition, her relatives yielding to her wishes to be at home, though those in charge of the institution warned them that she would probably die on her way there. However she did not die but lived to declare the wonderful works of God. When in awful agony and almost departing this life, the Lord appeared to her in a most wonderful vision. She says:

> It was as though the roof lifted and a most wonderful beam of light shone into my room. Then I saw the Lord in all His glory and this is what I heard, "Fear thou not, for I am with thee; be not dismayed, for I am thy God." Then I felt His touch on my arm, and heard His voice saying, "These are my words, take them, and believe them, and act upon them." The verses were James 5:14, 15. Three times I heard these words repeated to me.

In response to her call, seven Christian brothers and sisters gathered in her room, and after prayer and reading of the Word, carried out implicitly every command in James 5:14 and 15, anointing her with oil in the name of the Lord and praying the prayer of faith over her. Jesus again visited her in glory; she felt His hand on her head, her limbs were straightened out, and she felt a tingling, starting at her toes and reaching to her finger tips. The Lord spoke, saying, "Arise and get up." She said, "O Lord, I cannot." He spoke the second time, "Arise and get up — now or never!" She said, "O Lord, I will have it *now*." Then she received power to obey His command, jumped out of bed and walked around the room. Immediately she was perfectly restored to health and said, "Give me something to eat." Her deformed body was absolutely straight, and she ate two eggs and bread and butter and drank some tea with enjoyment. The next evening she walked one mile to a meeting.

The following certificate was signed by her attending physician, P. Eugene Giuseppe, M.B., C.M., J.P., formerly Government Medical Officer, Trinidad, British West Indies:

180 Kinnington Park Road, S.E.
April 15, 1921

I hereby certify that Edith May Cuffley has been under my professional care since December, 1917, and before that date under my predecessor, the late Dr. R. Foster Owen, for several years. She was rendered unfit for work in June, 1916, by reason of pulmonary tuberculosis, which was followed by spinal tuberculosis. She was more or less prostrated from that time until the 4th of April last, when she appears to have mysteriously recovered, having received no systematic treatment since her removal from a sanatorium in August, 1920. For the last two years she has been crippled, bed-ridden and believed to be incurable. In my opinion she is now recovered, and will soon be quite fit for work, and her cure can only be ascribed to her wonderful faith in prayer. (Signed.)

The following notes are from the pen of Dr. A. T. Scoffield, specialist, of Harley Street, London:

To my great pleasure I can record the case of Mrs. Cuffley, of 40 Denmark Road, Camberwell, S.E. After careful examination I must consider it a supernatural cure of organic disease. Mrs. Cuffley developed tubercle of the lung, had had hemorrhage, and lay in her bed for two years. X-rays showed advanced tubercle, and she was removed to the Home for Incurables and Dying at Thames Ditton. She lay in a spinal jacket and later on a water bed. . . . She has been nearly eight months perfectly well, walking about all day, visiting the sick and poor. I examined her chest and spine and there was certainly no active disease.

8

The Conquered Curse

Christ redeemed me from the curse of the law,
   As He hung on that shameful tree,
And all that is worse is contained in the curse,
   And Jesus has set me free.

Refrain:
Not under the curse, not under the curse,
   Jesus has set me free;
For sickness, I've health; for poverty, wealth,
   Since Jesus has ransomed me.

Christ paid the price of the broken law,
   He paid the whole price for me;
God saw not one spot, one blemish or blot,
   In the Lamb that was slain for me.

Do not abide in the ancient days,
   Ere ever the Lamb was slain;
Take that which was given as freely as heaven,
   And joined in the glad refrain.

From Deuteronomy 28, it is evident that disease,
all disease, is included in the curse of the broken

law. The following eleven diseases are specified as part of the penalty for disobedience to God's holy commands:

Blindness

Botch (perhaps leprosy)

Consumption

Emerods

Extreme burning (acute inflammation)

Fever

Inflammation

Itch (incurable form)

Madness

Pestilence

Scab

The Word further states: "Moreover he will bring upon thee all the diseases of Egypt, which thou wast afraid of; and they shall cleave unto thee. Also every sickness, and every plague, which is not written in the book of this law, them will the Lord bring upon thee, until thou be destroyed. And ye shall be left few in number, whereas ye were as the stars of heaven for multitude; because thou wouldest not obey the voice of the Lord thy God" (Deuteronomy 28:60-62).

It is related that Frederick the Great of Prussia once said to his chaplain: "Prove to me in one word that the Bible is a divine revelation." The chaplain replied, "The Jew, Your Majesty."

And surely nothing could be more stimulating to faith than a consideration of the unchanging faithfulness of God in fulfilling to His chosen people Israel every promise, whether of blessing or cursing. In a certain town in which I resided for some time, there was a synagogue. It was located in an obscure district, amidst unattractive surroundings, but was nev-

. ertheless a favorite place of pilgrimage for me. Not
that I ever entered it or took part in the worship
that was held there or even became acquainted with
the worshipers. No, I only stood and gazed and
gazed at the building, noted the date of its erection —
given in accordance with Jewish chronology — its
name, House of Jacob: "O house of Jacob, come ye,
and let us walk in the light of the Lord" (Isaiah 2:
5). And I noticed the strongly marked Hebrew characteristics of the faces of the attendants at the services. Once I caught a glimpse of a man robed in a
talith, or praying shawl. And as I looked, God's
Word, found in the chapter we are studying, words
uttered through human lips thousands of years ago,
would chant itself in sad, solemn strains in the very
depths of my spirit: "Because thou wouldest not obey
. . . ye shall be plucked from off the land whither
thou goest to possess it. . . . The Lord shall scatter
thee among all people, from the one end of the earth
even unto the other. . . . And among these nations
thou shalt find no ease, neither shall the sole of thy
foot have rest: but the Lord shall give thee a trembling heart, and failing of eyes, and sorrow of mind:
and thy life shall hang in doubt before thee; and
thou shalt fear day and night, and shalt have none
assurance of thy life" (Deuteronomy 28:62-66).

And the reason I loved to gaze at the synagogue
and the poor exiles from the Promised Land who worshiped there, was that I learned from their condition
— scattered among strangers who despised them —
the exactitude with which God fulfills His Word,
whether of blessing or doom. He permits us to see
with our eyes, and hear with our ears, the literal fulfillment of many portions of this 28th chapter of Deu-

teronomy; and history records the fulfillment with the most marvelous accuracy of many other portions. Take for instance verse 32: "Thy sons and daughters shall be given unto another people, and thine eyes shall look, and fail with longing for them all the day long: and there shall be no might in thy hand" (Deuteronomy 28:32).

In Portugal and Spain there were actually laws in force at one time that enabled anybody who was so minded to seize Jewish children and bring them up Catholics, which was esteemed a very meritorious action and one not infrequently performed by believers in Roman Catholicism. In such cases the Jewish parents were without recourse, had "no might" in their hands, as the Bible foretold. Look also at verses 49 and 50: "The Lord shall bring a nation against thee from far . . . as swift as the eagle flieth; a nation whose tongue thou shalt not understand; a nation of fierce countenance, which shall not regard the person of the old, nor shew favor to the young."

Perhaps the Roman standard which bore the eagle is referred to here; no two languages could be more unlike than the Hebrew and Latin, and the typical Roman countenance of the Caesar era is cruel and stern. Note verses 52 and 64: "He shall besiege thee in all thy gates." "He," first Nebuchadnezzar and later Titus. "And the Lord shall scatter thee among all people, from the one end of the earth even to the other." This has been literally fulfilled.

A converted Hebrew, the Rev. Mr. Schor, recently traveled extensively showing the present condition of the Hebrew race by means of exhibits which I carefully examined, finding among them photographs of Jews taken in all parts of the world. Chinese Jews wearing robes and queues, African Jews (many of whom were almost if not quite black in color) Russian Jews, Polish Jews, English Jews, etc., all partaking more or less of the characteristics peculiar to the countries where they resided.

If you ever have any doubts as to whether God always means *exactly* what He says, read with me verse 68: "And the Lord shall bring thee into Egypt again with ships . . . and there ye shall be sold unto your enemies for bondmen and bondwomen, and no man shall buy you."

This actually happened after the taking of Jerusalem by Titus. After the Jews had filled the measure of their rebellion against God by crucifying His Son, their Messiah and our blessed Saviour, their young men were shipped to the Roman works in Egypt and there sold as slaves; for so despicable were the Jews deemed at this time that Romans were actually ashamed to have them working for them as slaves, which was doubtless one reason for their transportation to Egypt.

I wonder how many of us feel that these instances are sufficiently numerous to convince us that God means just what He says in this 28th chapter of Deuteronomy. How many think so? Well, then we may feel sure that every other promise we find here, whether of blessing or of cursing will be as exactly fulfilled as the ones which we have examined. So we shall consider more, especially the ones relating to sickness and deliverance therefrom.

The Children of Israel, whom we have followed in their exodus from Egyptian bondage, Red Sea crossing, and wilderness wanderings, have now entered the Promised Land where they are immediately con-

fronted with two alternatives: the blessing and the
curse. The blessing would come by following obedience to God's commandments, which embraced every part of their beings and possessions — spirit, soul,
body, children (fruit of their bodies), cattle, crops,
and other possessions. It guaranteed them immunity
from all disease. "Blessed shalt thou be in the city,
and blessed shalt thou be in the field." Blessed ev-
erywhere, whether they went out or came in: "In
all that thou settest thy hand unto . . . the Lord
shall command the blessing upon thee. . . . The Lord
shall establish thee . . . and all the people of the
earth . . . shall be afraid of thee. The Lord shall
make thee plenteous in goods, in the fruit of thy
body, and in the fruit of thy cattle, and in the fruit
of thy ground. . . . The Lord shall open unto thee his
good treasure; . . . the Lord shall make thee the head,
and not the tail."

And the *curse* was consequent upon failure to
obey, which included every form of sickness and
disease which can attack humanity. In other words,
disobedience to God's law *puts* men under the curse,
which includes every form of disease. God is the
Lord who changeth not. A life of holiness is essential
to a life of physical wholeness; and both are ours
through faith in the Lamb of God (who was made a
curse for us) and can be obtained in no other way.
While I am far from depreciating the efforts that are
being made to stamp out sickness by scientific research, I say on the authority of God's Word that
such efforts can only be attended with a very limited
measure of success; for so long as sin exists, it will
— when it is finished — bring forth death, and disease is death begun. The latest statistics show a

greater mortality from cancer than ever before in the history of the human race in spite of all the work that has been done in millionaire-endowed laboratories.

Perhaps no more determined effort has ever been made by leaders among men than that which has been directed against the white plague, tuberculosis. I myself knew personally a most able man who spent eighteen years of his life in research work on this one disease alone. The results of his labors were contained in locked books, the contents of which were written in cipher. He was only one of an army of scientific explorers and investigators doing research on this disease. But in spite of their labors, tuberculosis still claims its annual quota of victims. And even if it could be completely stamped out, so long as sin still remains, it would inevitably be followed by sickness of some sort or other; for, as has already been said, "Sin, when it is finished, bringeth forth death." And disease is death begun.

So to be delivered from disease we must come to the One who settled the sin-and-sickness question for us on the cross of Calvary by being made a curse for us, and looking to the Lamb of God. Sing with grateful hearts:

Not under the curse, not under the curse,
    Jesus has set me free,
For sickness, I've health, for poverty, wealth,
    Since Jesus has ransomed me.

At one time I wondered that God saw fit to *specify* so many diseases in Deuteronomy 28 as part of the penalty for breaking His holy law, when it plainly states that all sickness — "every sickness and every plague, which is not written in the book of this law" — is included in the curse. But the Holy Spirit gave great light to me on this point when dealing with persons afflicted with some of the diseases so specified. Take tuberculosis of the lungs, for instance, commonly called consumption. I thank God that I have personal knowledge of many marvelous healings of this disease, which is so hopeless. I use the word advisedly, for while modern methods have undoubtedly done a great deal toward arresting its course in the earlier stages, there is still practically no prospect of recovery for advanced cases, excepting by faith in the work accomplished for soul and body on Calvary. And I know no better way of dealing with them than giving them the Word of God in the 28th chapter of Deuteronomy, along with some New Testament verses, more particularly Galatians 3:13: "Christ hath redeemed us from the curse of the law."

"There's no hope for me, doctor; I have consumption; three physicians have pronounced it tuberculosis of the lungs. I have been X-rayed and all the rest. They say it is quite advanced and the utmost I can expect is that my life may be prolonged somewhat if I am very faithful in following the instructions they have given me and in taking their remedies."

To which my answer is, "Do you believe that the Bible is the Word of God, and absolutely true in every particular?"

"Oh, yes; I know it is."

"Well, then, the Word of God explicitly states that Christ Jesus healed you of consumption, mentioning the name of the very disease from which the doctors tell you you are dying at this moment."

"Oh, where is it? I have never seen it in the Bible."

And then turning to Deuteronomy 28, I point out that consumption is part of the curse of the broken law, from which curse Galatians 3:13 tells us that Christ has redeemed us by being made a curse for us, or in our stead.

"Now repeat with me, 'Christ hath redeemed me from the curse of the law, of which curse consumption is a part, so Christ hath redeemed me from consumption.'" And the seeker obeys; and repeatedly, with the Bible open before us at Deuteronomy 28: 22 and Galatians 3:13, we say together, "Christ hath redeemed me from consumption." And faith cometh by hearing the Word of God, and the mountain is cast into the sea.

How thankful I am that God in His mercy and wisdom saw fit to include consumption, the great white plague, among the diseases specially mentioned in this category in the twenty-eighth chapter of Deuteronomy!

Let me relate in brief the history of a woman who was healed by the Word of God in my sister's ministry in our own home in Calgary, Alberta, Canada. I may say that later the sister received the baptism in the Holy Spirit, and has been a true witness for Jesus on all lines since her deliverance.

She is a trained nurse, and upon being pronounced tuberculous and made to live in a separate bungalow from the rest of the family and eat off marked dishes, she became very interested in the things of God. She had been saved some years before and came to our house in the hope of getting nearer to Jesus in her spiritual life. She had no hope of being cured of the disease from which she was suffering and wanted to be ready for the home call.

My sister was alone in the house when she called. After a little conversation which served to reveal the needs of the seeker, the Bible — in which the sick one implicitly believed — was searched, especially regarding healing. The twenty-eighth chapter of Deuteronomy and other verses were brought to her notice, with the result that she saw full salvation for her whole being, including her body, perfectly secured when Jesus was made a curse for her on Calvary. And she was immediately healed.

Some time afterward she was staying at the home of a prominent doctor who had a great esteem for her. He had not known her prior to her healing. One day, just for fun, my sister called him up and asked him if he saw any signs of tuberculosis of the lungs about the nurse he had in his family.

"Certainly *not*," he replied rather testily, and then he was told the wonderful story.

We are in constant touch with this nurse, hear from her at regular intervals, and know her life ever since her healing. It has been one of continual effort and sacrifice for others, a "poured out life," and there is never a hint of any recurrence of the dread disease from which she suffered.

It is noteworthy that among the diseases enumerated as part of the curse of the broken law are found some of the most malignant and virulent from which humanity suffers. Botch, for instance, is said to mean leprosy. Fevers are among the most dreadful scourges, especially in hot countries, such as typhus, typhoid, scarlett fever, smallpox, and other eruptive fevers. Blindness is one of the most awful afflictions from which any one can suffer, being only surpassed by madness, or insanity. The scab, an incurable form of itch, evidently refers to some of those awful and intractable forms of skin disease with which we sometimes come in contact.

How delightful to be able to say, on the authority of God's Word, Christ has redeemed you from *fever,* whether it be typhus, typhoid, scarlet fever, or small-pox; I can give you chapter and verse for it. Christ has redeemed you from *blindness;* for Deuteronomy 28:28 says it is included in the curse of the broken law, and Galatians 3:13 says that Christ redeemed you from the whole curse. Christ has redeemed you from that hopeless skin disease. The Bible says so.

I remember going out to a rather remote settlement with an evangelistic party comprising several workers. The girls were given a little house to live in, but the poor boy was taken to sleep with a game warden, who had a terrible skin disease from which he was seeking healing.

He told us the next day how sorely tempted he had been to refuse to sleep with the man. But how could he allow himself to be afraid of contracting a disease which he was telling the other fellow was part of the curse from which Christ had redeemed him? The devil said, "If you have to get into bed with him, keep all your clothes on, and you may escape contagion, though even then you will be taking terrible risks."

At first he was going to accept this suggestion, but the Holy Spirit lifted up a standard and said, "Can't you trust Jesus?"

And with that he said, "Yes, I can and do trust Him." And peeling off his clothes, he jumped into bed and slept as peacefully as an infant on its mother's breast. And the brother with the skin disease was perfectly healed. He always called his trouble itch, though it wasn't itch at all but something far more serious. I suppose it *itched* — it looked as though it would — and that was the reason he gave it the unpoetical name.

And it seemed as though we would never hear the last of his healing. Sometime a little later we were holding meetings in a fine Methodist church, where the large congregation contained many prosperous and refined persons.

In opening the service one evening I called for testimonies. Of course, I meant nice, polite testimonies, but who should jump up but Johnnie Hourie, the game warden. I didn't even know he was there, as it was far from his home, and he simply convulsed the audience by his testimony.

"Well, praise the Lord! He healed me of the itch!"

You should have heard them laugh! And you couldn't doubt his testimony. He made it very plain that he had suffered tortures, of which God had completely relieved him, in consequence of which he was bubbling over with gratitude.

And how glorious to be able to tell each sick one, no matter what the disease from which they are suffering, that Christ has redeemed them from it, even if it is not specified by name in this wonderful twenty-eighth chapter of Deuteronomy; for we are told in verses 60, 61 that all diseases, without a single exception, are included in the curse.

9

The Bible or Christian Science

The Bible or Christian Science — which shall it be? You cannot have both, for they are opposed to one another on all essential points.

"But I thought that Christian Scientists recognized the Bible and are diligent students of it," someone says.

They may read the text, especially portions of it and carry a copy of it, along with *Science and Health with Key to the Scriptures,* but they do not receive it as the Word of God in truth, eternal, immutable, forever settled in heaven. For on page 139, lines 20 and 21, of their official textbook, we read: "A mortal and material sense stole into the divine record, with its own hue darkening to some extent the inspired pages." And of a statement of the Holy Ghost, in Genesis 2:7, "The Lord God formed man of the dust of the ground," Mrs. Eddy does not hesitate to say (you will find it in the third paragraph of page 524 of the *Key to the Scriptures*: "How could a material

organization become the basis of man? . . . Is this
. . . real or unreal? Is it the truth, or is it a lie? . . .
It must be a lie." (All quotations are from the edi-
tion of 1917.)

Much of Christian Science literature is vague and
difficult to understand, but whenever anything essential is stated clearly, it is found to be absolutely an-
tagonistic to the Scriptures.

Sometimes people ask, "What is the difference between Christian Science and divine healing, as taught
in the Bible?" They have *nothing* in common. The
false philosophy on which Christian Science is found-
ed denies that Jesus Christ is come in the flesh, that
His body was a real body, and it is therefore anti-
Christian.

The Bible teaches healing as coming to us through
the atoning work of Christ on Calvary, with which
Christian Science does away altogether; for, according to Mrs. Eddy's teaching, since there is no sin,
there can be no redemption.

"But do they not have healings?" I believe, from
the Bible, that they do; for we are taught to expect
to see miracles wrought by satanic power, especially
toward the end of the age. But the infidelity which
they teach is so fatal that I feel about their healings
like a woman who sent a request for prayer for her
son to a meeting I was holding in a Methodist church
in Oakland. "My son is terribly sick," she wrote,
"there is no human hope, but I ask you to pray for
his healing to the God with whom all things are possible. But let none but those who believe in the precious blood of the Lamb as our only approach to God
pray for my boy. Let no one who does not honor

the Blood touch my suffering boy by so much as a thought."

Dr. A. B. Simpson was one of the most well-balanced men spiritually I have ever met, and he says of Christian Science, "I would rather be sick all my life with every form of physical torment, than be healed by such a lie."

"Open confession is good for the soul," and I feel impelled to relate just here a bit of my personal experience (which I much prefer to keep to myself) and to say that if anyone ever *tried* to believe Christian Science I was that person.

As I have already told you in an earlier chapter, I wakened one morning to the realization that I was in a hopeless quagmire of drug addiction, from which nothing human could extricate me.

I had tried everything that medical science could suggest, had been discharged from the hospital as a patient they could not help, and had taken the Gold Cure. After spending practically all I had, impoverishing my poor mother and other relatives as well by my ceaseless efforts to find relief from some source, I turned to my neglected Bible and my interrupted prayer life. And very soon the light on healing began to dawn upon me from the cross of Calvary.

As I felt a faint flutter of hope in my breast — where all had been for so long the stillness of despair — I turned to older Christians for encouragement, and not one crumb of comfort did they give me. Remember this was over twenty-six years ago. As I read and re-read the Bible, I saw more and more clearly that not only was provision made for our healing but that we were ourselves commanded to go forth and in the name of Jesus lay hands on the sick and heal them. I said, "I will go to some of the believers I know and point these verses out to them, and ask them to pray with me that I may be healed." And I started on my weary rounds.

I was so desperate that I knew no shame in presenting my petition. No rebuff was stinging enough to make me desist. Some said, because they were ashamed to confess that they did not believe the Word of God: "We are too busy to deal with your case today. Some other time, at the prayer meeting perhaps, you might ask for prayer."

And I would reply, "Nothing you can possibly be doing is as important as complying with Jesus' last command to you to lay hands on the sick that they may recover. Pray with me right here and now and I believe God will heal me."

But they would not, and at last I said, "The Bible says, 'These signs shall follow them that believe,' and as they don't follow these professed Christians, evidently they are not believers. It is said that they follow Christian Scientists, that they heal the sick, so they must be believers, and I will appeal to them." I went to New York City and got in touch with the leaders of the work there.

Through the influence of a friend who stood very high in Christian Science circles (she was afterwards a prominent practitioner in Berlin), I secured treatments from a most eminent Scientist, then practicing in New York. Of course I paid a goodly sum for them; but it was a great favor to get them at any price, and I was made to feel that I was under the greatest obligations to all who had assisted me to do so.

Of course I purchased all their literature, and at

the command of my practitioner plunged up to the neck in *Science and Health,* reading it every waking moment, or nearly so, very rarely allowing myself a dip into Mrs. Eddy's *Miscellaneous Writings.* I was told that there was absolutely no trouble about my morphine addiction and the awful physical conditions which had resulted therefrom; that it did not really exist and would vanish like snow wreaths before the sun as soon as I freed my thoughts from its "self-imposed materiality and bondage" by absorbing enough of *Science and Health.*

> I had a fall, I broke my arm, wherever should I go?
> A Christian Science doctor shall dissipate my woe.
> I found the lady calm and sweet, for it was office hours,
> And she on absent treatments must concentrate her powers;
> You think she felt the broken bone? No, nothing half so tame,
> She looked into the distance and just denied the claim;
> "In mortal error you are swamped but truth you now shall see,
> For as you have no arm to break, no arm can broken be.
> Since all is good, and good is all, just voice the truth and say,
> 'My arm is strong, and sound, and whole.' Ten dollars, please. Good-day!"
> I said, "Because in light and truth you're plunged up to the neck,
> Just say, 'I have ten dollars now, and thank you for your check.'"

That sounded good to me, you may believe, and I simply devoured Mrs. Eddy's book. Although I did not know the Bible then as I do now, I felt something like the man whose experience I read some time ago. He was told by a woman friend that what he needed was to study *Science and Health with Key to the Scriptures,* by Mrs. Mary Baker Eddy.

"Why, I didn't know the Scriptures were locked; but if they are, it is a mighty lucky thing the lady found the key," he replied.

"Yes, it is the greatest blessing that has ever befallen humanity," said his friend.

And she was so enthusiastic that he finally consented to read the Bible with her. She obligingly opening it with the wonderful "key."

"Mother used to teach me the Bible," he said, "and it seems as if I would enjoy visiting some of the old rooms in it. Take me to the one where we learn about how God created man and man disobeyed God and fell."

"Oh, this is a very wonderful book. And you must be prepared for some surprises, delightful ones all of them. That room you speak of is closed, for Mrs. Eddy has discovered that God did not create man, for 'God and man co-exist and are eternal' (page 336, line 30, (*Science and Health*), and also that 'Whatever indicates the fall of man . . . is the Adam-dream . . . not begotten of the Father'" (page 282, lines 28-31).

"Lead me to the incarnation room where we are brought face to face with the ineffable mystery of the Word made *Flesh,* the Holy Spirit coming upon the virgin, the power of the Highest overshadowing her, so that the Holy Thing that was born of her, Christ Jesus, was true God and true man."

"Well, I must prepare you for changes there, for 'Those instructed in Christian Science have reached the glorious perception that . . . the virgin-mother conceived this idea of God and gave to her ideal the name of Jesus'" (page 29, lines 14-18, *Science and Health*).

"But if Jesus was only an 'idea' how could He say to His disciples after the resurrection, — you will find it in Luke 24:39, — 'Behold my hands and my feet that it is I myself; handle me and see; for a spirit hath not flesh and bones, as ye see me have'?"

"Oh, don't let that trouble you at all. Mrs. Eddy explains it away beautifully. Just listen to these marvelous words of wisdom — you will find them on page 313, lines 26-29, of *Science and Health* — 'To accommodate Himself to immature ideas of spiritual power . . . Jesus called the body, which by spiritual power He raised from the grave, flesh and bones.'"

"Well, if you don't mind, I think I will keep out of that room for there is a verse that says, 'Every spirit that confesseth not that Jesus Christ is come in the flesh is not of God: and this is that spirit of antichrist. . . . Receive him not into your house, neither bid him God speed: for he that biddeth him God speed is partaker of his evil deeds' (1 John 4:3; 2 John 10, 11). Take me to the room where Jesus Christ is evidently set forth crucified, His own self bearing our sins in His own body on the tree, by whose stripes we were healed, where the Blood, which cleanses from all sin, and brings us nigh to God, by which we have boldness to enter into the holiest, is extolled."

"I cannot, for that room is closed forever to all believers in Christian Science."

"Closed? What do you mean? The Bible says in Hebrews 9:22, 'Without shedding of blood is no remission.'"

"Yes, but Mrs. Eddy has made the glorious discovery, which has much to do with the wonderfully rapid increase in our membership, that there is no need for remission of sin because there is none to be remitted. She has taught us the 'Nothingness of sickness and sin' (page 347, line 28), that 'sin, sickness and death' are 'a dream' (page 188, line 12). Isn't that a blessed release? Just believe it and see how comfortable you will feel!"

"I don't seem to get much comfort out of it for a scripture that mother taught me, 'If we say we have no sin, we deceive ourselves, and the truth is not in us' (1 John 1:8), will keep floating through my consciousness, try as I may to drown it. Perhaps I had better pray for light. The Bible says, 'Ask and ye shall receive' (Matthew 7:7)."

"To what purpose? We are taught in *Science and Health* that prayer to a personal God is a hindrance. On page 3, we find this question: 'Shall we ask the divine Principle . . . to do His own work?'"

"So you are taught to think of God as a Principle merely. Well, it seems to me that there isn't much left of the Book after the lady that found the "key" gets through with it."

And that was the way I felt as I studied the textbook, but I was so determined to be *healed* that I tried to shut my eyes to its blasphemous heresies and to swallow it holus-bolus.

My practitioner was a lady with exquisitely beautiful hair, which was always so artistically puffed that it seemed there was not so much as a single hair out of place. She was placid as a summer sea and assured me in the sweetest, calmest way possible that my sin and sickness were only bad dreams from which

I should shortly awaken to find everything all right. And at last I really began to half believe it. Like Jonah, I was sinking, down, down, down, down; and like Jonah, I was saved by the direct intervention of God.

I made up my mind to go on with the thing and see what it could do for me. But God had other plans for me, and He sent a whale — it was a big one — to swallow me.

One morning I awakened to find that complete paralysis of the right arm had come on during the night; and as I am not in the least ambidextrous, it would be hard to find anyone in a worse predicament than mine.

Of course I rushed to my practitioner to find her wholly undisturbed by the catastrophe. How could she be disturbed when she knew that not only had I no paralysis of the arm but no arm to be paralyzed? She never turned so much as a silver hair but assured me that "There is no life, truth, intelligence, nor substance in matter. All is infinite Mind and its infinite manifestation, for God is ALL in ALL. Spirit is immortal truth; matter is mortal error. Spirit is real and eternal; matter is unreal and temporal. Spirit is God and man is His image and likeness. Therefore man is not material; He is spiritual." This clearly proved, as you will no doubt perceive, that I had no arm and therefore could not have paralysis in it.

Whether or not I had an arm, there was one thing that I didn't have: money. And I was so sure of it that I didn't need to resort to Christian Science to tell me that I didn't have it. I couldn't stay in New York in my helpless condition without money. There was room rent in a very expensive house just off Central Park. There was the high fee charged for treatments. Living in the area was extremely high, so I had no alternative but to return to my home in Winnipeg, Canada.

Indeed, I thought it advisable to leave immediately before any of my other limbs went out of business. So I said a farewell to my practitioner, who was still floating on a summer sea up to the last glimpse I had of her; and having fortified myself with Christian Science literature to enable me to continue my treatment after I reached home, I left.

And there God provided just what I needed. An old friend, an aged minister of the gospel whom I deeply reverenced, was sent from a far land to minister to me. His heart went out in Christ-like sympathy when he beheld the havoc Satan had made in me, the utter destruction of everything that could make life worth living. He did not chide me when he saw me clinging to *Science and Health,* but he did say, and most solemnly, "Sister, that book is straight from hell, and the first step you must take to get deliverance is to burn it."

He did not argue but he prayed — prayed, I believe, without ceasing; I know of one whole night he spent in prayer for me. And at last one day I staggered down to the kitchen; I was almost too weak to stand upright, but I deposited my copy of *Science and Health* on the glowing coals. It is the only proper place in the universe for it.

Not very long afterwards the light of the glorious gospel of Christ for soul and body shone into my heart. And the drugs with the resultant diseased conditions vanished like snow wreaths, not because they had not been real but because Jesus Christ who died and rose again to deliver me from them is real. They were *real* sin and *sickness,* but in Him I found a *real* Saviour able to save to the uttermost.

To recapitulate, the Word of God, which "endureth forever," and *Science and Health,* produced by Mrs. Mary Baker Glover Eddy, are diametrically opposed on all essential points; so we have to choose between them. Which shall it be then, the Bible or Christian Science?

10

Forever Settled

"Forever, O Lord, thy word is settled in heaven" (Psalm 119:89). "My word . . . that goeth forth out of my mouth . . . shall not return unto me void, but it shall accomplish" (Isaiah 55:11).

Ralph Waldo Emerson said, "No accent of the Holy Ghost this heedless world hath ever lost," which is true; not that the heedless world has safeguarded the priceless treasure, but that the Word of God can't be lost. "It abideth forever" (1 Peter 1:23). It is incorruptible seed; frost will not kill it; the sun cannot scorch it. It liveth, and behold! it is alive forevermore. It is not only true; it is truth: "Thy word is truth" (John 17:17).

"Where the word of a king is, there is power" (Ecclesiastes 8:4), and where the Word of the King of kings is, there is omnipotence. In order to make that almighty Word operative in us and for us, one thing only is necessary and that is to believe it.

The Word of God is with us today, for it cannot

be lost. It is just as omnipotent as it always has been and always will be. It is incorruptible, so it cannot suffer change of any kind. We have but to make connection with the batteries of heaven by pressing the button of faith to have the exceeding greatness of God's power revealed in our lives.

It is possible we have all read the story of the blowing up of Hell Gate in New York harbor, an engineering feat which was considered very remarkable at the time of its performance a number of years ago.

When it was decided to remove the dangerous rocks which had caused the loss of many ships and precious lives, large gangs of men were set to work to honeycomb them with drills. When the drilling was completed, powerful explosives were placed in position, and the whole was wired and connected with batteries located many miles away.

When the hour announced for the explosion arrived, the chief engineer was in his office in New York City with some officials and his staff of assistants. On his knee sat his tiny granddaughter and in front of him on his desk was an insignificant looking key, or button, by means of which little Mary was to blow up Hell Gate.

How it was to be accomplished she had not the remotest idea; that was Grandpa's business, but that it would be done she could not doubt, for had not Grandpa said so; and with perfect confidence that, as she did it, those gigantic rock masses were splintered into fragments and scattered to the four winds, just as Grandpa had told her, she pressed the button with all her might. Far away in the distance a dull booming sound was heard, and in a moment the message was flashed over the wire, "Hell Gate is no more."

The touch of a child's finger in obedient faith in her Grandfather's word unlocked the forces which his wisdom had provided for the demolition of the frowning obstacles; but the touch, feeble as it was, was requisite. Though everything necessary to the clearing of the channel was finished, the child's finger had to release the power.

Do you understand the allegory? God's Word of full salvation for spirit, soul, and body, eternal and glorious deliverance for the entire man has been spoken; nay, is being spoken, for *it liveth* and back of it is Omnipotence; but we, children as we are, must press the button with our tiny fingers. When God's people do this in its fullest sense; the message will be flashed to heaven, "Hell's Gate is no more." And the day is coming when this will happen, for we are told that the gates of hell shall not prevail against the church. This does not mean that we are merely to defend ourselves against Satan's aggressions, but that we shall march against his gates and demolish them.

In Luther's time the enemy had the harbor of peace with God so blocked with dangerous rocks that many were lost in their attempts to make it. With all their penances, fastings, pilgrimages, scourgings and grovellings before popes and priests, perhaps comparatively few in his day knew what it was to be free from condemnation before God; the way was a veritable "Hell's Gate." But by believing the Word, "The just shall live by faith," "To him that believeth on Him that justifieth the ungodly his faith is counted for righteousness" (Romans 1:17; 4:5), Luther pressed the button. Omnipotence was brought into action, the channel was cleared, and countless myriads sailed safely into port and proved for themselves that "being justified by faith we have peace with God through our Lord Jesus Christ" (Romans 5:1).

The Word regarding our bodies is just as express as that concerning our souls. Jesus healed the sick and said, "Thy faith hath made thee whole, go in peace." And the way into healing, and wholeness is just the same today, for He is the same; and if anyone will be small enough and humble enough and trustful enough to obey Jesus as exactly and simply as little Mary obeyed her Grandfather, we shall have an explosion of divine power one of these days that will shatter the rocks and clear the channel into the harbor of perfect soundness through faith in His Name.

Thank God for what He has done, but "there's more to follow," as the old hymn says.

God's Word regarding healing is "forever settled" and it has always been made living and real in exact proportion to the degree of faith exercised by His people. To show that this statement is amply borne out by recorded facts, let us briefly review the history of divine healing from the earliest ages to the present time, dwelling a little on the work of some of the more modern exponents of this truth.

It is a noteworthy fact that there is in every religion that has ever existed some belief, either clearly expressed or tacitly implied, that the healing of the human body is part of the function of the god or gods worshiped by the followers of that creed. One writer, the president of a university, says that the fact that the healing of the sick has been mixed up from time immemorial with religion has most seriously hindered the development of medical science.

I believe that the widespread existence of this belief is due to the common origin of mankind, and the retention — to some extent at least — by all peoples and races, of the original revelation of God to our first parents. This includes the fact that sickness is the result of sin and that the Supreme Being, whose law has been violated, is the only one who can effectively deal with it. I further believe that the healing of disease is "mixed up with religion," as the writer I have quoted puts it; because God has joined them, and what God hath joined together man may not put asunder.

History shows us the ancient Babylonians, Chinese, Egyptians, East Indians, Greeks, Romans, as well as other races, having recourse to religious observances, sacrificed to their demon deities prayers and various other ceremonies in case of sickness; but writing about the Jews, one historian states, "Disease was considered a punishment for sin, and hence the cure was religious rather than medical."

From the foregoing it is evident that it has been the general conviction of mankind in all ages that sickness has a spiritual origin and requires divine power for the remedy; even the heathen in their benighted way bear witness to this truth. So far from being a modern fad, as it has sometimes been called, divine healing is the ancient and original method of dealing with our inherited ills, even among heathen peoples. Among God's chosen people, the Jews, nothing else seems to even have been thought of until after the reign of Solomon during which so much that was idolatrous was introduced.

It was prophesied of the Christ some 700 years

before His first advent by the prophet Isaiah that He
would bear not only the sins of the world but their
infirmities and sicknesses as well on the Cross, which
word He fulfilled, healing all that were oppressed of
the devil and commissioning His followers to carry on
the work after His ascension, promising to be with
them until the end of the age.

In the Book of the Acts of the Apostles we learn
how literally they understood and how faithfully they
executed this command; and at least for the first
three centuries of the church's history their example
was closely followed by believers on the Lord Jesus
Christ.

Listen to the following quotation from one of the
best known fathers of the Early Church, Irenaeus,
dated about A. D. 180, as he draws a comparison between heretics and true believers on the Lord Jesus
Christ.

> They [the heretics], can neither confer sight on
> the blind, nor hearing on the deaf, nor chase away
> all sorts of demons . . . nor can they cure the weak,
> or the lame, or the paralytic; or those who are dis-
> tressed in any other part of the body. Nor can they
> furnish effective remedies for those external acci-
> dents which may occur, and so far are they from
> being able to raise the dead, as the Lord raised them,
> and the apostles, and as has frequently been done in
> the brotherhood, the entire church in that particular
> locality entreating with much fasting and prayer the
> spirit of the dead man has returned in answer to the
> prayers of the saints — that they do not even believe
> that this could possibly be done.

In another place he says: "Others again heal the
sick by laying their hands upon them and they are
made whole. Yea, moreover, as I have said, the dead

even have been raised up, and remained among us for many years."

The great Christian father, Origen, wrote in the third century of the Christians of his day:"They expel evil spirits and perform many cures . . . Miracles are still found among Christians, and some of them more remarkable than have ever existed among the Jews; and these we have ourselves witnessed." These statements would have been challenged by Origen's opponents if they had admitted of being disputed.

It would appear that praying for the sick and anointing them with oil never ceased to be practiced for the first seven centuries of the Christian era, though after that it began to decline as the result of the changed attitude and apostasy of the church. But in spite of this, many notable healings took place after that date; and the fact that as superstition became rife it was usual to connect these with the name of some saint or other instead of giving all the glory to Him to whom it rightfully belongs — our blessed Jesus — does not invalidate the fact that the healings, which were prayed for in the name of Jesus, actually occurred.

Perhaps these people did not grieve the Lord any more when they connected their healings with the prayers of Saint Solemundygundus or some other saint or a relic of Saint Ann or a piece from the Virgin's robe than we do when we think that if this brother or that sister prays with us, we shall be healed, instead of placing all our confidence in Jesus alone.

That the healings actually occurred, all historians are agreed; and as one of them, not a religious writer, says, if we refuse to believe it we may as well decline to accept the whole historical record, for they are as well attested as any part of it.

In the beginning of the 12th century we find Bernard of Clairvaux (France), author of the famous hymn, "Jerusalem, the Golden," a leader of Christian thought in his day. He was a man eminent for holiness of life, mightily used in healing the sick, 36 miraculous cures being reported as taking place under his ministry in a single day — the halt, the blind, the deaf, the dumb being perfectly restored in answer to his prayer in the name of Jesus. One one occasion a dying man was brought to him who was so emaciated that his legs were no larger than a child's arms, and when Bernard prayed, "Behold, O Lord, they seek for a sign, and our words avail nothing, unless they be confirmed with the signs following," and laid hands on the living skeleton in the name of Jesus, the sick man arose from his couch healed.

Toward the close of the 13th century, an Englishman, called Thomas of Hereford, was much used in healing; documentary evidence, which is still extant, shows that no fewer than 429 miracles of healing were performed by him through laying on of hands in the name of the Lord Jesus Christ. Though it occurred long after his death, his faith and teaching seem to have inspired the trust in the Word of God that brought the following miracle to pass at the beginning of the 14th century. I quote from the original account of the occurrence:

> On the 6th of September, 1303, Roger, aged two years and three months, the son of Gervase, one of the warders of Conway Castle, managed to crawl out of bed in the night and tumble off a bridge, a distance of twenty-eight feet; he was not discovered un-

til the next morning when his mother found him half naked and quite dead upon a hard stone at the bottom of the ditch, where there was no water, or earth, but simply the rock which had been quarried to build the castle. Simon Waterford, the vicar who had christened the child, John de Bois, and John Guffe, all sworn witnesses, took their oaths on the Gospel that they saw and handled the child dead. The King's Crowners [coroners], Stephen Ganny and William Nottingham, were presently called and went down into the moat. They found the child's body cold and stiff, and white with hoar frost, stark dead. While the Crowners, as their office required, began to write what they had seen, one John Syward, a near neighbor, came down and gently handled the child's body all over and finding it as dead as ever any, prayed earnestly, when the child began to move his head and right arm a little, and forthwith life and vigor came back into every part of his body. . . . That same day the child, feeling no pain at all, walked as he was wont to do up and down in the house, though a little scar continued in one cheek, which, after a few days, quite vanished away.

I used to be very much puzzled at the reports I read in the course of my studies in history of the healings of hopeless cases of tuberculosis, then called "scrofula" or "king's evil" (some of them signed by eminent doctors of the age in which they were stated to have occurred), as the result of the king's touch. These patients were carefully examined by court physicians before being allowed to present themselves for the king's touch. The screening was necessary because some who were not grievously afflicted were anxious to be touched and to receive the small gold coin which it was the custom for the king to give to those to whom he ministered in this way and which was worth far more than its intrinsic value; and in some instances these very doctors solemnly attested that the people had been perfectly cured. When I came to look into the matter I found to my great surprise that the ceremony was a solemn religious one based on the words in the last verses of Mark's Gospel. "In my name . . . they shall lay hands on the sick and they shall recover," and that this verse among others, was read aloud to each person who sought healing; also that the king prayed as he touched the sufferer, in which prayer his chaplains and all bystanders were supposed to join. In view of these circumstances it is no wonder that real healings took place in some instances, through the power of the Word operating on souls and bodies.

Indeed the reports of some of these healings are so convincing that I cannot doubt for my part that the boundless grace of God found a way to honor the Word and magnify the glorious name of Jesus, even though the instruments employed were not always all that might have been desired.

King Edward the Confessor, who was a real Christian, prayed for a young woman whose case is very striking. The woman was afflicted with large abscesses in the neck. The king placed his hands gently on the diseased tissues, stroking it as he prayed for her recovery. The abscesses opened, discharging tremendous quantities of putrid matter filled with maggots. Within a week no trace of the disease could be found.

With the Protestant Reformation came a revival of faith for healing, and the tide has been gradually rising ever since that time. These believers are just a few God has used in the healing ministry: Martin Luther; George Fox, founder of the Quakers; John

Wesley; Charles G. Finney; Dorethea Trudel, whose work became so extensive that it was investigated and finally in some sense licensed by the Swiss government; Dr. Charles Cullis of Boston; A. J. Gordon; Dr. A. B. Simpson of New York; Mrs. Carrie Judd Montgomery, formerly of Buffalo, New York, later of Oakland, California; Mrs. Elizabeth Mix of Connecticut, a black woman through whom Mrs. Montgomery was healed; John Alexander Dowie of Zion City, Illinois; Dr. William Gentry of Chicago; and Mrs. Aimee Semple McPherson. Many other names stand out in this connection as we pass the centuries in review.

It has been my privilege to know personally some of these men and women. And in passing I should like to dwell for a few moments on recollections of two of them who have passed to their reward, Dr. John Alexander Dowie and Dr. A. B. Simpson.

I met Dr. Dowie in about 1900. He introduced himself to us and dwelt on the meaning of his name: "John," by the grace of God, "Alexander," a helper of men. As for the "Doctor," it had been bestowed upon him by grateful people who were healed in answer to his prayers. While I could never fully follow Dr. Dowie in all of his teachings, I could not doubt the truth of his statement that God had conferred upon him gifts of healing. The Holy Spirit answered to it in my soul, and he was approved of God by miracles and wonders and signs which God did by him, which the very man in the street could neither gainsay nor resist.

For instance, I once asked one of the very best dentists in Chicago what he thought of Dr. Dowie. He did not know that I had any acquaintance with him. He replied, "Well, it is impossible to deny the genuineness of his healings; how he does them I cannot explain, but he does them without the shadow of a doubt. I myself know a young lady who had her leg lengthened three inches, and who now stands on even feet. You can see her any Sunday in Dr. Dowie's choir."

When Dr. Dowie began his work in Chicago, in 1893, I think it was, he set up a wooden hut at the World's Fair and rang a dinner bell to get the people to the meetings. This is history. He had some wonderful healings, among others that of Ethel Post, a little girl of about 13 years of age whose mouth was so full of a bloody, spongy cancer that she could not close it day or night. The surgeons would not touch it for fear she would bleed to death, for the blood vessels in it were so infiltrated with cancer cells that they would not hold ligatures. As Dr. Dowie drove across Lincoln Park to pray with her, the Lord gave him the verse that He is God to kill and make alive (2 Kings 5:7), and he prayed, "O Lord, kill the cancer and heal the child."

The malignant growth withered away and fell out of her mouth and throat, and she was completely and permanently healed. When I alluded to her case in a meeting quite recently, a lady rose and stated that Miss Post is alive and well and actively engaged in some branch of commercial art. She used to sell her photographs, "Before and After the Lord's Healing Touch," for the benefit of the Lord's work, and they in themselves constituted a wonderful testimony to the faithfulness of God toward those who trust Him.

I visited at Dr. Dowie's Divine Healing Home in 1898; it was then on Michigan Boulevard, Chicago, and was a most luxurious hotel fitted up in approved modern style. But it had something I had never seen in any other hotel: a staff of helpers all of whom were filled with faith in the Word of God. Their faces shone, and any one of them — from the furnace man to the elevator boy — was ready to preach you a sermon at a moment's notice if you dared to doubt that Jesus Christ is the same yesterday, today, and forever.

Dr. Dowie's devotion to the Word of God was beautiful; he would read it to his sick folks for hours on end, sometimes not even stopping for dinner; and as he read they would visibly lift up their heads like flowers after a gracious shower. I have known him to put dinner back when it was served and the waitresses waiting to attend the tables because he said we needed the Word so much more. He simply brought you right up against the Word, "I am the Lord that healeth thee," and expected you to believe it then and there without any regard to symptoms.

One of his favorite hymns, which we sang very frequently, was a sort of keynote to his character and work. I will quote part of it here; and if you are familiar with it, you will notice that he altered it to suit himself:

> Have God's own faith
> And trust his might,
> That He will conquer as you fight,
> And give the triumph to the right,
> Have faith, have God's own faith.
>
> Have God's own faith
> What can there be
> Too hard for Him to do for thee?
> He gave His Son, now all is free,
> Have faith, have God's own faith.

Dr. Dowie had invincible, God-given faith in the Word of God as being the same today as it ever has been and ever will be, "forever settled," absolutely supreme and unconquerable, "whose faith follow." If there was anything in his life or teaching that you do not see to be in accordance with God's Word, you are not called upon to follow it; but his faith in God's Word you are exhorted to imitate.

It was hopeless organic disease of the heart which threatened to end Dr. A. B. Simpson's life in the very midst of his career of usefulness as a minister of the Gospel that brought him to a knowledge of the truth of divine healing. When he was in such a condition that there was constant danger of his falling from the pulpit or into the open grave as he officiated at funerals, Dr. Simpson was ordered by his physician to stop work and take a prolonged rest. He was given but little hope that he would survive long, no matter what precautions he took. He was earnestly looking to God when the truth was revealed to him through the Word.

Without the faintest improvement of any kind in his symptoms, he took God at His Word and believed himself healed, ever after acting on this through a long and most arduous life of service. God never failed to meet his physical need; and eternity alone will tell the story of the work accomplished in practically every country of the world by this faithful soldier of the Cross, for the great burden of his soul was world evangelization in preparation for the coming of the King.

In a little verse he wrote, which I shall quote, is found the explanation of the great work which by divine grace he was able to perform:

I am crucified with Jesus,
  And He lives and dwells in me;
I have ceased from all my strugglings,
  'Tis no longer I but He.
All my will is yielded to Him,
  And His Spirit reigns within;
And His precious Blood each moment,
  Keeps me cleansed and free from sin.
I'm abiding in the Lord,
  And confiding in His Word,
And I'm hiding, sweetly hiding,
  In the bosom of His love.

All my sicknesses I bring Him,
  And He bears them all away,
All my fears and griefs I tell Him,
  All my cares from day to day.
All my strength I draw from Jesus,
  By His breath I live and move,
E'en His very mind He gives me,
  And His faith, and life, and love.

Dr. Simpson had some wonderful healings in his
ministry. Only a few days after he accepted Christ as
his physician, his little daughter, their only child, was
taken with malignant diphtheria. Her throat was
filled with awful membrane and her condition was
most critical. He took her out of her mother's arms and
into a room where he was alone with God, and there
anointed her with trembling hand. She was only the
second or third person he had ever anointed. He
knew that unless God manifested His power quickly
there was going to be a crisis in the family, for his
wife was not at that time one with him on the subject
of healing.

All night he knelt beside the child in prayer. And
when with the first streak of dawn the mother entered

the room with haggered face and eyes heavy with weeping, the little one opened her eyes and smiled at her, the smile of health and happiness; and not one vestige of the dread disease remained. "All Hail the Power of Jesus Name!"

11

Signs Following

"Now when Jesus was risen early the first day of the week, he appeared first to Mary Magdalene, out of whom he had cast seven devils. And she went and told them that had been with him, as they mourned and wept. . . . Afterward he appeared unto the eleven as they sat at meat, and upbraided them for their unbelief and hardness of heart, because they believed not them which had seen him after he was risen. And he said unto them, Go ye into all the world, and preach the gospel to every creature. He that believeth and is baptized shall be saved; but he that believeth not shall be damned. And these signs shall follow them that believe; In my name shall they cast out devils; they shall speak with new tongues; they shall take up serpents; and if they drink any deadly thing, it shall not hurt them; they shall lay hands on the sick, and they shall recover. So then after the Lord had spoken unto them, he was received up into heaven, and sat on the right hand of God. And they went forth and preached every where, the Lord working with them, and confirming the word with signs following" (Mark 16:9, 10, 14-20).

Here we have in the plainest possible words God's program for the age in which we are living — a program in which every believer has his or her appointed part to play. It is not too much to say that we are here simply and solely for this purpose, for we are ambassadors for Christ, as though God did beseech by us, "be reconciled to God." As faithful ambassadors we have all the resources of heaven to draw upon, and Omnipotence to empower and protect us.

I have worked under the government and know what it is to receive instructions, often by telegram, directing that certain changes be made, new regulations promulgated and enforced; and as these were complied with the government invariably confirmed them by official letters bearing the great seal and by such action as might be necessary to ensure the discharge of all governmental obligations in connection therewith. I do not remember that they ever failed to confirm their word, perhaps they did. But the Government of Heaven never fails to make the Word of God good in every respect, to fulfill every promise contained therein and to inflict every penalty threatened for disobedience thereto; for the Lord Himself is working with us, confirming the Word with signs following. So we can be absolutely certain that if we speak as the oracles of God, as we are directed to, He will not let any of our words fall to the ground but will confirm them with signs following, setting the seal of heaven on our utterances.

As we proclaim salvation from sin and deliverance from its guilt and power through the cross of

Calvary, men and women will have their shackles
struck off before our eyes; and as we preach a Saviour
who bore our pains and sicknesses as well as our sins,
the sick will be healed, the deaf will hear, blind eyes
will be opened, the lame man will leap as a hart,
and the tongue of the dumb sing.

If the puny governments of earth cannot afford to
let their utterances go unconfirmed, is it likely that
the King of kings will allow His eternal Word to be
unfulfilled? It is unthinkable.

I am going to relate a few instances which have
come under my personal observation of the confirma-
tion of the Word of God by the signs following — with
the view first of glorifying Jesus, and second of in-
spiring faith in the hearts of those who hear them, or
of increasing and strengthening it if it has already
been inspired.

People sometimes speak as though the healing of
the body through faith in the Sacrifice of Calvary were
something quite distinct from salvation, instead of
part and parcel of it. Let us look for a moment at the
case of the paralytic who was brought to Jesus by four,
in the fifth chapter of Luke. Here Jesus first speaks
the word of pardon — first things first: "Man, thy sins
are forgiven thee," after which follows his physical
healing as a visible sign of his forgiveness and an
evidence before the eyes of all of the power on earth
of the Son of man to forgive sins.

Jesus desires to convince the unbelieving world
of the reality of His gospel by His healing miracles
on the bodies of the sick who come to Him for deliverance. Often in this way a door of utterance is
opened for the heralds of the Cross which would

otherwise remain closed; and the first incident that I shall relate is an illlustration of this.

Just before leaving Canada for California, my sister and I received an urgent call to hold meetings in a rural part of Alberta. We had to drive a long way in a car to get there — it was a considerable distance from the railway — and the roads are not like the ones in California. We seemed to have to pray the car along almost every foot of the way, partly because the roads were bad and partly because the car was none too good. However, we got there at last and were soon hard at work holding meetings in schoolhouses and homes, visiting the sick, tarrying with seekers for the baptism in the Holy Spirit, and doing other work that came to hand; and we had the joy of seeing God move in a blessed way.

Finally we felt that we were free to return to complete our arrangements for going south, so we bade them all a loving farewell and told them to have the famous car ready for an early departure the following day. Quite late the last evening we expected to spend there, a man called to see us, bringing his wife and family. He was an unbeliever and I noticed that one of his children, a little boy, had a marked squint in one eye. I told the parents that it was not God's will that the little thing should be so deformed and afflicted and that we would pray for him if they wished. As they replied in the affirmative we laid hands on the child in the name of Jesus, and then they went home. I cannot remember that I noticed any change in the eye directly after we prayed, but as we were very busy seeing people who came to say good-bye, it may have escaped our notice; in any case, early the next morning before we had finished breakfast the man returned and reported that the child was so improved that they were all amazed and recognized God's hand in the healing. He implored us to stay a while longer and promised to come and bring his family to the meetings if we would do so, which meant something as he lived a long distance from the place where we held them.

As he added that he and his family were ready to make an unconditional surrender to the Saviour who had healed the child, we decided that the happening was a token from the Lord that He still had work for us to do there. We announced that we would continue the meetings, inviting all who were really seeking the baptism in the Holy Spirit, but *no others,* to come to a tarry meeting in the upper story of our host's barn that very evening. It was a wonderful barn, the finest one in the whole district. And I certainly shall never forget that meeting; it was in some respects the most wonderful one I ever attended.

As I was on my way to the meeting, I saw a man with a most unhappy expression on his face, skulking in the distance but casting longing glances all the same toward the huge, gray barn. I called to him and asked him if he wanted to come to the meeting.

"Yes," he said, "I want to come but I am too bad a man. I am known all over this district as a bad man. My wife is at the meeting; she is a godly woman and I have led her an awful life. I am a bad man."

"Well," I said, "you are the kind the meeting is for, for the worse you are the more you need Jesus; and we are going to seek Him there tonight as Saviour, Healer, Baptizer, and All in All. Come along."

So the "bad man" (we'll call him John) accompanied me to the meeting. Maybe the people were astonished to see him come in, but that was as nothing to the astonishment that was to fill them a little later.

The people knew almost nothing about the Baptism; and as they were from various churches and societies, I explained the way of full salvation in the simplest manner possible, including the baptism in the Holy Spirit as in Acts 2:4 and told them to look to the Lamb of God and praise Him for all He had procured for them. And they began. Everybody expected John's wife to receive the Baptism first. I found that she was considered the best person in the district.

I can see those people now if I close my eyes. It was a beautiful loft, a real "upper room," the floor covered with new mown hay and the whole place lighted by lanterns hung round the walls. The faces of the seekers looked so earnest in the flickering lantern light. There was a spirit of love and harmony, for all who were not seeking the Baptism were asked to stay at home.

John knelt on the outside of the ring where the shadows were deep as the lantern light hardly penetrated to that distance. I wondered how he was getting along and intended going to pray with him; but before we had been on our knees many minutes, the power fell and a sister — not John's wife — received her Baptism. As she was kneeling next to me she fell over on me and I could not get away.

When John's wife actually heard this sister praising in other tongues, she seemed to grow desperate in her longing and began with all her might to call upon God for the Baptism.

I was encouraging her when suddenly as a flash

of lightning the power of God struck John where he was kneeling, bolt him upright at the edge of the group, and felled him to the floor with a crash so mighty that it seemed as though it must pull the building down. And he lay there under the power, which moved and manipulated every part of his body with such force and lightning — like rapidity that the people thought he was having an awful attack of convulsions. Indeed it was with great difficulty that I calmed their fears. At last the Spirit began to speak through him, first in English, describing the vision he was having of Calvary. Would to God that every sinner in the world could have heard him! It would have melted a heart of stone. And after that he spoke with awful power and majesty in a new tongue.

His wife was so dumbfounded when she heard him that she said to me: "He's got the Baptism before me and he was *so* bad. Perhaps I need to be saved from my goodness more than he needed to be saved from his badness."

And I said, "Perhaps you do. Just repent of everything and cast yourself on Jesus."

And just then, to the amazement of all, John raised himself to his knees and came along to us, and placing himself in front of his wife, he preached the most wonderful sermon on Calvary I ever heard.

"Oh, look away from yourself, bad or good," he cried. "See, where *He* hangs bearing your sins away forever and making your peace with God — everlasting peace, sure as Jehovah's throne!"

It was thrilling. He seemed to see Jesus and to be able, through the power of the Spirit, to make us see Him too.

As he kept pointing her to Calvary, the power

caught another sister up as though on a whirlwind; and she danced all round the loft lighter than a feather — she had never seen dancing in the Spirit — praising and singing meantime in Gaelic. Later the language changed to High German, which I had studied for years and understood a little; and she was unable to speak anything else for a couple of days. When spoken to in English, she replied in German. She had no knowledge of the language.

A sister who was taking charge of her baby — he had awakened by this time — asked for his bottle and she danced all round the loft looking for it but unable to stop dancing and singing.

Meantime the power was falling on others and there were days of heaven on earth, and the salvations and baptisms came about through the healing of the child's eye. It is pretty hard to separate healing from salvation, isn't it? For my part I have given up trying.

I am now going to relate another healing which we always called, "The man borne of four," because he came in the light of that verse in Luke 5 which was referred to earlier in this chapter.

He was an old man between 70 and 80 years of age with a cancer on his face, on the temple near his eye. Sometimes people say that the diseases of which we claim to be healed are imaginary, but they could not say that about this case; for he had a face and he had a cancer on that face. He was not at all a good-looking old man and with this hideous growth he presented a most repulsive appearance. As far as you could see him you would notice it; and, unless you were very careful, you were likely to exclaim, "Isn't that awful!"

The old man was genuinely saved and was quite willing to bear the affliction until he was called home, if God so willed. But as he listened to the teaching from the Word he became more and more certain that Jesus had purchased his full deliverance on the cross of Calvary and more and more determined to have that deliverance manifested in his mortal body.

As he considered himself weak in the faith, he asked God to give him some special help and was directed to request four sisters, whose prayer joints were kept well oiled, to carry him to the feet of Jesus as the bearers carried the paralytic. Nothing loath, they accepted the task and performed it so faithfully that the cancer simply dropped off and vanished forever.

It seemed to me that it went so quickly that it was there one day and gone the next; but I know there was an interval between the prayer and his manifested deliverance, though I cannot say exactly how long it was. God enabled them to fight the good fight of faith during it anyway, and the disappearance of the cancer was a grand testimony for Jesus in that town; for no one could deny that Grandpa had had a cancer, and no one could find a trace of it after his healing. I have heard him preach an eloquent sermon on the Lord's healing with the cancer for a text more than once, and I have never heard anyone attempt to dispute his statements.

The next case of which I shall speak was one of blood poisoning following childbirth, and the woman who was healed was actually dying when the miracle occurred. I mean that she was in the very article of death. Indeed, I could not find the faintest trace of a pulse when I laid my hand upon her. I had taken a long drive to reach her, and as it was raining and we were in an open vehicle, rivers of water were pouring from my slicker; but her husband insisted on my going in without a moment's delay, saying when he met us at the door with a face as white as chalk that she was just passing away.

As I felt the immediate presence of death and the power of darkness rolling like a flood, over the woman, who was perfectly unconscious, the Spirit of the Lord within me raised up a standard against the enemy. I could not have done it; I was too scared, and through my lips came the words, "The prayer of faith shall save the sick, and the Lord shall raise him up, and UP YOU COME"; and at the same instant she opened her eyes and spoke to her husband (who was bending over her weeping, never expecting to hear her voice in this world again). "Don't cry, sweetheart; Jesus is here" — she had a vision of Him — "and has healed me." She was so occupied with Jesus and His beauty and sweetness that she did not even know that I had been there until after I left. I met her some little time afterwards on the main street of the town on a shopping trip with a flock of curly headed little ones after her; and she was certainly very much alive.

The last case I call "The Story of Samuel," not the Samuel of the Bible but another Samuel who was named after the Samuel of the Bible because he was, like him, a child of faith.

This husband and wife were godly people who had a good, comfortable home with the benediction of God resting upon it but no children to brighten it and inherit the blessing promised to the seed of the righteous. This was a great grief to them, especially as the woman suffered a great deal at the hands of physicians who endeavored unsuccessfully to remove, by means of painful operations, the trouble that prevented her from bearing a child. But, alas! Like the woman in the Gospels, she grew worse rather than better, and the only results attained were physical debility and suffering and large doctors' bills. She was getting well on in years when she and her husband received the baptism in the Holy Spirit and a fresh illumination on the sacred page. With this came a conviction that barrenness and disease were not God's will for her but part of the curse of the broken law which Jesus had borne in her stead when He was made a curse for her. She prayed that the blessing of Abraham, which includes fruitfulness, might come upon her and was determined to prove God and see if He would not open the windows of heaven and pour out upon her the blessing of motherhood.

So we gathered around her, a little praying band of earnest people, and with her took our stand on the unchanging Word. So real was our part in the matter that when the child arrived (he had to arrive, for the Scripture cannot be broken), we with one accord named him Samuel, saying with Hannah, the mother of the Bible Samuel, "For this child I prayed." All of us felt that he belonged to us quite as much as to his father and mother. We used to set him in our midst, and gloat over him; and when a year and a half later the Lord graciously sent him a little sister just for good measure, she was called Ruth (completeness), and our cup of rejoicing was full.

But what shall I say more? Space would fail me to tell of the sick I have seen healed of almost every disease that flesh is heir to: the goiters that have melted away; the blind that have been made to see; the deaf to hear; the lame to walk; the cases of tuberculosis; heart disease; kidney disease; indigestion; gall stones (one Roman Catholic woman who had pulmonary consumption and gall stones was instantly healed on her deathbed after receiving Extreme Unction, and then the Holy Spirit fell upon her at the same time so that she praised God for her deliverance in a new tongue); tumors of various kinds (including cancer, which have been perfectly cured; sometimes instantly when hands were laid on and prayer made in the name of Jesus).

A woman who was healed of cancer of the breast in our home in answer to prayer seemed to constitute herself a publicity agent for the Lord's healing. Every now and then our phone would ring and somebody would say when we answered it, "Do you remember Mrs. Campbell who was healed of cancer in your house? She told me that if I would ask for prayer in Jesus' name I would be healed too."

Yes, the signs follow. God always confirms His Word. Step out upon it this minute, whether for yourself or others, without a tremor. It has never failed and it never will fail, for they that trust in the Lord shall never be confounded.

12

Teaching, Preaching, and Healing

Among the last words uttered before the closing of the Old Testament canon, before the sad, silent centuries which intervened between Malachi and the first coming of the Lord Jesus Christ (by whom God hath spoken to us in these last days), we find predicted the rising of the Sun of Righteousness with healing in His wings (Malachi 4:2). This prediction was fulfilled when Jesus, the Dayspring from on high, visited us; and as He was manifested to destroy the works of the devil — including sickness as well as sin — He healed *all* that came unto Him, *all* that was oppressed of the devil.

And, thank God, He is still the Sun of Righteousness with healing in His wings and is beaming love, forgiveness, cleansing, and healing on all who will let the blessed Sunshine — the life which is the light — into our hearts and lives. "Clear the darkened windows, open wide the door, let the blessed sunshine *in.*"

It is hard to keep sunshine out. Even when you have drawn every curtain close, pulled down the blinds, locked the shutters, and shut every avenue of approach, it has a way of stealing in and making a spot of glory in the midst of the gloom. And God is not willing that any should perish; and even when the doors are barred against Him, He loves us so much that He is always sending some ray of divine light through the prayers of His people or their testimonies or their loving smiles or some Word of God dropped into our minds by the Holy Spirit to lighten our darkness and to invite us to throw our whole beings wide open to the illuminating, warming, electrifying, healing, energizing, vitalizing, magnetizing, rays of the Sun of Righteousness.

I saw some little children once who were the very incarnation of health. They were nutbrown from head to foot, and they radiated physical vigor and well-being from every pore. I asked their mother, "What have you been doing to them?" And she replied, "I had them at the seaside and it was beautiful weather; just sunshine all the time. And I stripped off their clothes and put tiny bathing trunks on them so there wasn't a thing between them and the sunshine, and the sun did all the rest. Dr. Sun is my doctor from henceforth."

Yes, the sun is a wonderful doctor, but even he sometimes fails; but the Sun of Righteousness never fails to illuminate the darkest heart that is opened wide to receive Him and to heal the most hopeless case that comes to Him. Only we must be like the tiny children; we must have nothing between us and the Sun; not so much as a cloud to arise and darken our skies or hide for a moment our Lord from our eyes, nothing of sin or self that could separate us from Jesus.

Shall we open wide the doors and windows? If they are already open, throw them wider; or better still, step right out of ourselves into Christ. As a song in the Spirit which the Lord gave to my sister, says:

> Step out into the light, and stay there,
>   Walk there, sit down there;
> Step out into the light, and grow there,
>   Praise the Living Word;
> In Jesus all is bright, so live there,
>   Rest there, abide there;
> Step out into the light,
>   Pass on through faith, to sight,
>   The light of God.

Now let us take a look at the work of Jesus, the Saviour and Healer, as described in the New Testament. Note first of all He followed a definite method and order in its performance: (1) teaching, (2) preaching and (3) healing (Matthew 4:23). "First things first," so Jesus first teaches; He reveals to man God's will for him and shows him how far he has wandered from it. Second, He preaches or proclaims to man the salvation provided for him through Christ Jesus, which, accepted by faith, brings him into perfect harmony with the divine will. And third, heals; He removes from human bodies the results of sin. This is God's order, and it is well to remember that it is unchanging.

Sometimes people who come to be healed of some distressing complaint are likely to feel rather impatient when — instead of at once praying for their immediate deliverance — we deliberately, prayerfully, and reverently, read to them from the Word (even for hours if the Spirit so leads). They forget that the words themselves are "Spirit and life" and that "He sent his word and healed them."

I have seen patients who were so completely drained of vitality that, from a medical standpoint, I should have thought it necessary to administer powerful heart stimulants at frequent intervals to prevent collapse. But they listened to the Word of God for hours continuously and lifted their heads under the distillation of its heavenly dews like a parched garden after a gracious shower.

The Word *teaches*, reveals God to man, so that man abhors himself in dust and ashes. As Job says, "Now mine eye seeth *thee*. Wherefore I abhor myself and repent in dust and ashes" (Job 42:5, 6). *Preaches,* shows him the way out of defilement into holiness, by the blood of Jesus — "Having therefore, brethren, boldness to enter into the *holiest* by the blood of Jesus" (Hebrews 10:19), and *heals all* who will through the boundless grace that flows from Calvary, accept God's perfect will for spirit, soul and body, "that they may be preserved *blameless* unto the coming of our Lord Jesus Christ" (1 Thessalonians 5:23).

When Jesus said to the impotent man in the fifth chapter of John's gospel, "Wilt thou be made whole?" He meant nothing short of this. Not only that his poor atrophied body should rise from its supineness but that the whole man should rise to walk in Heaven's own light, above the world and sin; for in the 14th verse of the same chapter we find Him telling the man to sin no more. It is God's revealed will toward us not only to remove all sin and disease but to lift us far above the realm in which sin and disease operate, even into the Resurrection Life of Christ: "The law of the spirit of life in Christ Jesus hath made me free from the law of sin and death" (Romans 8:2). And He is saying to each one, "Wilt thou be made whole? Not *half*, not 60 percent or even 90 percent, but 100 percent, whole!"

So much for a general consideration of the teaching of the New Testament regarding healing. Now we will study some particular cases found in the eighth chapter of Matthew.

The first thing that strikes us as we begin is the fact that each case in the New Testament has certain features peculiar to itself, not to be found in connection with others. I believe that this is to show us how inexhaustible are God's resources and how perfectly able He is to meet the need in each case that is unreservedly placed in his hands.

The first patient in the eighth chapter of Matthew is the leper who believed implicitly in the *power* of the Lord to heal him but doubted His *willingness*. "Lord, *if thou wilt*, thou canst make me clean (Matthew 8:2). Jesus, the author and finisher of faith, completes the supplicant's faith by His "I will," and the result is the man's immediate healing.

The Bible, from Genesis to Revelation, is God's "I WILL" to every seeker for full salvation for soul and body. Jesus, the only begotten Son of God, hanging on the cross in agony and blood, is God's "*I have* delivered you, and this is what it cost me. Can you doubt My willingness?"

Jesus speaks of healing as "the children's bread" in the 15th chapter of Matthew, and no earthly father worthy of the name will withhold bread from his children, much less our Heavenly Father.

We are taught to pray, "Thy will be done on earth as it is in heaven"; and there is no sin or sickness in heaven, for nothing that defileth can enter there.

God desires our bodily healing just as He desires our spiritual well-being, for the apostle John prays for the well-beloved Gaius, "Beloved, I wish above all things that thou mayest prosper and be in health, even as thy soul prospereth" (3 John 2).

Some say that this leper was told not to testify, but that is a mistake. Rather he was directed just how, when, where, and to whom, he was to testify. He was to testify to the priest, the official appointed to examine lepers and pronounce them clean in the event of their healing; and he was to bring the required offering. One reason for this was that leprosy is a type as well as a result of sin, and the righteousness which is by faith of Jesus Christ is to be witnessed to by both the law and the prophets (Romans 3:21). After I was healed of the morphine habit some of my Christian friends begged me never to mention the fact that I had been a drug addict. But the Lord told me to show what great things He had done for me, even if it humiliated me to do so; and He told me just when, where, and how, I should testify. Shortly after I was delivered I went to a church in Chicago, a Methodist church, and as soon as opportunity was afforded for testimony, I rose and told what a marvelous deliverance God had wrought in me.

After I sat down a young man stood up in the back of the church and said that he praised God for my testimony, for it gave him courage to tell what God had done for him. He had been a hopeless drunkard and had been completely delivered and gloriously saved. His friends had begged him to keep quiet about it (he belonged to a wealthy family), but my example so inspired him that he declared he was going to testify for Jesus every chance he got; and preach Him too, for he felt called to preach. And I heard him give a splendid sermon that very evening at the hall of the Volunteers of America.

After the service in the Methodist church a gentleman walked up to me and introduced himself as Dr. William Gentry. He was in medical practice in Chicago then. He told me how impressed he was with what I had said, the truth of which he could not doubt. Later he gave up the practice of medicine and devoted himself to the Lord's work from that time.

The next case in this chapter in Matthew is that of the Roman centurion who sought healing for his servant, who was delivered in answer to his master's great faith. Note that the centurion asked for nothing but the word: "Speak the word only"; and also observe that he did not base his request on any merit in himself. "Lord, I am not worthy . . . speak the word." I believe that if we could and would divest ourselves of every vestige of self-righteousness and settle it once and for all that we in ourselves are worthy of nothing but eternal doom (but that the Lamb of God who was slain for us, Christ Jesus, in whose name we come, is worthy to receive "power, and riches, and wisdom, and strength, and honor, and glory, and blessing") we would witness signs and wonders such as have not as yet gladdened the eyes of men.

One of the most prompt deliverances I ever witnessed was that of a young ballet dancer who had an awful attack of appendicitis and had been ordered to the hospital for an operation. And I believe that one secret of her instantaneous healing was the fact that she knew, as did everybody else, that she had nothing in herself to recommend her to God. It had to be "all Jesus."

She was just a wicked, flirting, swearing, smoking sinner who had to cast herself in self-despair at the feet of Jesus; and He taught her that way and brought her that way, "Lord, I am NOT worthy . . . speak the healing word." And He spoke it, and in one minute after that she had no more need of an operation for appendicitis than I have this moment. She was a perfect little heathen when I first met her, and she was transformed into the most earnest advocate of the Lord Jesus as the healer of His people that I have ever known.

The next case in this chapter is the healing of Peter's mother-in-law (Matthew 8:14, 15), in which I call Jesus the *family* Physician.

Here there does not seem to have been any special question to settle prior to the healing, as in some other healings recorded in the Word. Peter, the head of the family, had accorded to Jesus the rightful place of preeminence, and He enters the home and banishes the works of Satan from the premises. Luke tells us (he was a physician, remember) in correct medical phraseology that she was suffering from a "great fever," following the teaching of the famous ancient Greek physician, Galen, who divided fevers into lesser and greater. But as the sufferer, with flushed face and aching head, tossed uneasily on her bed of pain, Jesus drew near and touched her hand and the fever left her; for vital contact with Christ banishes disease. "Some one hath touched me," and by vital continuity with Him we are delivered from the power of sin and sickness and quickened by resurrection life (Romans 8:2, 11). As the result of her healing, Peter's mother-in-law arose, took higher ground — every one who is healed by faith in Jesus does that — and ministered unto Him (Matthew 8:15, margin). We are saved and healed to serve Him.

It is a glorious thing to have Jesus as our family Physician, and no one is too poor to secure His services; for they are "without money, and without price." Let me tell you a true story of what He did for a little girl whose father and mother placed their home under His almighty care and keeping.

At a tent meeting in western Canada at which I was one of the workers, a sweet little five-year-old girl, whose ears had been destroyed by the ravages of scarlet fever, was brought to the altar by her mother to be healed of deafness.

The child was so deaf that it was impossible for her to hear any sound, no matter how loud; and there was no prospect, humanly speaking, of any improvement in her condition. I asked the mother, who led the child to the altar, if the father was saved; and on receiving a reply in the affirmative, I asked him to come with his wife and child and definitely receive Jesus as the family Physician, claiming perfect spiritual and physical deliverance for all under the rooftree through the power of the Blood upon the door.

> I'll sing it, yes, and I'll shout it!
> The blood! the blood!
> There was never a soul saved without it,
> THE BLOOD OF CALVARY.

After they had unitedly and publicly taken this stand, the child was anointed and prayed for in accordance with James 5:14, 15, and left in the hands of the family Physician. The meeting was a very large one and I never happened to see her again. But some months after returning to our home, we received a beautiful feather pillow (I really think it is the finest one I ever saw in my life) as a thank offering from the mother for the child's complete recovery, with the statement that she could hear a pin fall. We handed the pillow over to my own little adopted daughter; and as she laid her head on it every night for years, the fact that it was an offering from a little girl who had been healed of deafness was a constant inspiration to her faith in Jesus as the family Physician.

Well, perhaps you say, "But my case is quite different from any of those you have cited. It is not like the leper's, nor that of the centurion's servant, nor Peter's mother-in-law. How can I be sure from this verse that there is healing for *me?*"

If that is your feeling, turn to the 16th verse of this same chapter where we read, "They brought unto him many . . . and he cast out the spirits with his word, and healed all that were sick." "All that were sick" — He healed all that were *sick.* How many did he heal? All, no matter what kind of people they were or what the nature of the diseases from which they were suffering, whether acute, sub-acute, chronic, functional or organic. He healed all that were sick. All. You cannot get outside of that, can you? So bring your case to Him now, singing:

> Just as I am without one plea,
>   But that Thy blood was shed for me,

And that Thou bidst me come to Thee,
O Lamb of God, I come.

And you will go away not only healed in body but in
soul also; for Jesus removes not only symptoms but
the deep-seated cause of symptoms, sin in the heart,
which no remedy but the Blood can reach.